The
WOODLAND
BOOK

The
WOODLAND
BOOK

101 ways to play, investigate, watch wildlife
and have adventures in the woods

BLOOMSBURY
LONDON · BERLIN · NEW YORK · SYDNEY

For my tree mate Duncan

This book contains some potentially dangerous activities to be undertaken in the natural environment. Trees and woodlands are prone to changing conditions throughout the year and in response to changing weather conditions. The author and publisher have endeavoured to ensure the accuracy of the information herein. The author and publisher cannot accept any legal or financial responsibility for any accident, injury, damage, loss or prosecution resulting from the information, use or misuse of the activities, techniques and advice in the book. Any reader taking part in tree climbing, swinging, whittling or any other activities does so entirely at their own risk.

Published 2014 by Bloomsbury Publishing Plc, 50 Bedford Square, London WC1B 3DP

Copyright © 2014 text by Tessa Wardley
Copyright © 2014 illustrations by Tessa Wardley
Copyright © 2014 in the photographs Tessa Wardley except as listed below.

ISBN (print) 978-1-4729-0000-5
ISBN (epub) 978-1-4729-0002-9

A CIP catalogue record for this book is available from the British Library

This book is produced using paper that is made from wood grown in managed sustainable forests. It is natural, renewable and recyclable. The logging and manufacturing processes conform to the environmental regulations of the country of origin.

Design: Nicola Liddiard, Nimbus Design

Printed in China by C & C Offset Printing Co Ltd
10 9 8 7 6 5 4 3 2 1

We are grateful to the following for permission to use their copyright photographs:
Shutterstock: **p.41t** AnimalPhotography.ch, **41bl** Bildagentur Zoonar GmbH, **41cr** Erni, **41bl** H Fuchs; **p.43tl** Borislav Borisov, **43bl** Vitaly Ilyasov, **43r** jack53; **p.45t** Mircea Bezergheanu, **45c** Fernando Sanchez, **45b** David Dohnal; **p.47** IbajaUsap; **p.79br** craigbirdphotos; **p.80tr** Vishnevskiy Vasily, **80obr** Borislav Borisov; **81r** Tadas Naujokaitis; **82** Vishnevskiy Vasily; **83** Mircea Bezergheanu; **107br** Kirsanov Valeriy Vladimirovich; **135** Kelvin Wong; **162t** Jool-yan, **162c** Portokalis; **163** Eduard Kyslynskyy; **164** Bildagentur Zoonar GmbH.

Contents

Introduction

Entering a wood is like opening a book. The leaves fold back and invite you on a journey into the unknown, a green tinged anticipation of shadow and light. Crossing the threshold you discover a mosaic, a dream world pulsating with new life and ancient wisdom, rich in magic and mystery.

When I was nine my grandparents stopped farming their smallholding in Norfolk and my parents planted a woodland on a few acres of their land. Illogically, as the fastest growing member of the family, I was used as the measuring stick for those young trees and every few months I was photographed in amongst them to register their progress. The dry, sandy soil of Norfolk was not the easiest place to grow trees, our weekends were spent nurturing them; wading through the knee high grasses and stripping them away from the engulfed saplings in an effort to give the youngsters a competitive advantage. Rabbits also love the sandy soil and it was a constant battle to keep their gnawing teeth away from the succulent young stems. We did, and still do, employ a local ferreter to keep the rabbit numbers down a bit but it is a genuinely Sisyphean task. Each time he visits he will catch upwards of 200 Rabbits in a weekend. One time I saw him he suggested we should just admit defeat, accept the forces of nature, rename the place 'The Warren' and be done with it.

However, over the years the trees prevailed. There now stands a proud, young woodland perfect for my children, their cousins and friends who all enjoy climbing, investigating, den building, camping and generally having fun. The wildlife is enjoying the woodland too, deer lie up in the bottom corner, fraying the trees as they rub off their antler velvet, a family of foxes have a den and the rabbits still abound; their gnawing can be seen on the trunks and new stems but most of the trees are mature enough to withstand their attention.

I now live in the most wooded county in England – Surrey – and almost every day I have the opportunity to walk, run, climb, have mini adventures in the woodlands or even just sit and contemplate. Throughout the writing of this book I have taken that opportunity and my trusty companion is my boundy, young, flat coat retriever, Alfie, who never knows what the day will bring.

Some days I take my camera and walk. There are frequent stops as I rummage in my backpack and Alfie bounds over, ears up, the desire for food always strong and his goldfish memory ever hopeful. You can almost hear the sigh of resignation as he sees the camera come out; the ears go down and his shoulders visibly slump as he folds to the ground, sphinx-like, waiting for me to move on again.

On other days we go for a long trail run. One such day my friend Vanessa and I decided on a woodland run in an attempt to escape the sideways rain that threatened to pincushion us. Up on Ranmore Common the billowing spears of rain drenched us before we had crossed the 200m of open ground to reach the woods. A winter broadleaf woodland doesn't provide the best protection but at least the rain was falling from its traditional position above our heads rather than driving in from the side. We hunkered down and splashed though puddles and squelched through the drenched leaf litter. Our feet danced

between the tree roots, avoiding the temptation to stand on them, when your feet just glide off the sides and leave you on the floor. There had been so much rain that the trees were frothing. Running down their flanks, as on exhausted racehorses, streams of foam gathered around their base. Poor Alfie didn't get a chance to so much as roll in a fox poo as we dashed along the trails between the austere rain-blackened megaliths; sinister but invigorating. Back in the car the three of us steamed and shivered, clouding the windows, we were elated by our mini-adventure; a good towel rub and steam by the Aga was calling.

On other days I just like to sit and contemplate. A passer-by glancing into the monochrome stripes of the young birch and Ash would be surprised to see me swinging gently in my hammock seat hanging from an arched Ash tree, Alfie leans heavily against my legs, both of us silently watching, listening, absorbing our surroundings without moving. The late winter sunlight, the first for what seems like months, slices through the bare canopy and a line of vast upright beech trees wearing electric green leggings on their solid legs, like an elephantine corps de ballet, look for all the world as though they may just haul their roots from the ground and march off to do battle with the forces of evil like Tolkien's Ents.

Probably the best days for Alfie are the family days. We walk a bit, there is invariably food involved, there are lots of people and often other dogs to play with, at some point we are bound to stop in a nice interesting area with lots of distractions. There is plenty of time to pursue smells, have a little dig and generally investigate

without getting left behind. People often hide and have to be found, there is lots of screeching and sometimes people fly through the air on ropes. Most exciting is that there is lots of bounding and barking to be done then.

As a species humans have an interesting relationship with the woods. Since we swung down from the branches long ago in our evolution we have maintained a spiritual, cultural and physical dependence on trees.

The Chinese know wood to be the fifth element, sustained by its relationship with the other four elements: earth holds it roots, the fire of the sun feeds it, the wind plays music in its leaves while water ebbs and flows within. In Norse mythology the Ash tree – Ygdrasil – is the tree of life with its roots in the underworld and branches in the heavens, this is echoed closely by the 'World Tree' of the ancient Celts and many

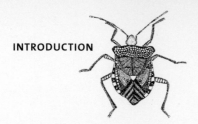

other ancient cultures. Throughout the world human beings rely on wood to construct homes and as a source of heat and cooked food; our very lives depend on the woodlands around us as they exchange carbon dioxide for oxygen giving us clean air to breathe. At Kew Gardens recently I found a plaque which informed me that two mature trees provide enough oxygen for a family of four.

Emotionally woodlands are symbols to us of all that is ancient and stable, they are our history and our wisdom. You just have to look at an old oak tree; vast, craggy, and whiskered, its twisted limbs draped in a blanket of mosses and lichens to see the central role it plays in nature. It is an ancient, venerable being; the wise old man of the woods, all seeing and all knowing. Conversely the woods are also perceived as places of mystery and fear where hidden forces are at work. I have carried out a little survey amongst friends and whichever emotion woodlands invite: tranquillity, contentment, security, excitement, fear, wonder or awe, our feelings on woodlands are rarely neutral. We all feel some emotion towards woodlands and now it is my opportunity to try to enhance that emotion.

Writing this book has allowed my family to have many adventures, we have fallen further into love with woodlands and have become more and more curious and discovered more about the woods than I would have imagined possible. My youngest daughter has an aversion to me teaching her anything. I am not a teacher and I clearly don't warrant the time of day when I attempt to impart some small nugget of knowledge. However, I am allowed to play. Richard Mabey (2010) claims that we are never closer to nature than when we are playing. Play is intricately linked with art, both are fed by our curiosity and by the same virtue curiosity is the basis of all science.

While I hope to pass on some information about woodlands I believe the most important gift a book can give to anyone is curiosity. If I give you some knowledge, it is finite; you will soon reach its end, but curiosity is a gift for life. I hope this book contains some useful information, but more than anything I hope it instils a curiosity and a desire to find out more about woodlands and to love them a little better.

There are woodlands all over our beautiful islands and in the interest of knowledge I would be delighted if you had a go at relaxing, playing, being creative and having adventures in woodlands. It is time to get out there and be curious.

How to use the book

If you are a little at a loss with woodlands the introductory section of the book will explain a little about woodlands, their ecology as you see them today and how they got where they are. If you need help finding your local woodlands read through the section on 'Finding woodlands'; there are literally thousands of woodlands of all shapes and sizes throughout the country and every one is either listed on a website or marked on maps. So, arm yourself with a map and you will be set to get out there and find your own woodland haven.

Within the rest of the book there are six sections full of activities to suit the way you feel, whether you want to relax, play, make something, investigate, have an adventure or answer some questions.

Each activity starts with a journal extract where I convey the images that I captured and that engaged my imagination. In most cases this is followed up with 'how to' sections that give more detailed information, which should enable you to try out or refine the activities that may or may not be familiar to you. Where relevant there are also notebook sections which provide all sorts of information about woodlands – the wildlife, geography, mythology, natural history or just stories that will enrich the experience.

The underlying philosophy of this book, if there is one, is one of simple curiosity. Strip out all the unnecessary clutter of life, just go down to the woods for the day and have fun with what you find. You don't need bags of specialist equipment. There is always something around trees on which to build a game, investigation or adventure without the need for hours of planning and bags of kit.

Visiting woodlands is a fantastic way to get out into the great outdoors, challenge the ties of technology and get some fresh air, a bit of exercise, nourish your senses and be inspired. The fact that it is easy on the pocket and the environment is a bonus.

The Woodland Book will give you the confidence to side-step the 'work hard, play hard, walk fast' mentality; to indulge your inner ape, and just go to the woods for the wood's sake. Revel in the freedom, feel a little wild and feed your curiosity. It is free, simple, environmentally-friendly and therapeutic.

Getting started

A bit about woodlands

Woodland history on Britain's shores began as the ice retreated at the end of the last Ice Age. Trees re-colonised the bare glacial soils to develop our wildwoods.

The exact nature of our post-glacial wooded land is unknown. It has been assumed, that before neolithic man got involved, the whole land was a dense wildwood, however, Rackham (2006) believes it may be more likely that our natural state would have seen islands of wildwood interspersed with open grazed land. Whatever the reality in prehistory, today Rackham identifies 'woodlands' as land with trees growing closely such that their canopies meet. Many trees also exist in 'wood pasture' where the trees are more widely spaced and interspersed with grazing land – grassland or heather.

In this book I am largely considering woodlands and wood pasture following Rackham's definitions above. Wild trees and particularly ancient trees are often not contained in woods but stand alone around buildings and in

hedgerows, and at times I will also make reference to these islands and corridors of tree ecology.

Another important distinction when discussing woodlands is the definition of ancient woodlands. Alongside the wild woods in this country we have a history of plantation that is believed to have begun around 1600. Any woods known to precede this date are deemed to be 'ancient woodlands'. Ancient woodlands are particularly important because of their long history in situ; they grow on undisturbed land and while they may have been extensively managed they have reproduced and grown naturally. The richness and diversity of the wildlife associated with ancient woodlands is unrivalled in any other UK habitat.

Other designations of woodland you may come across include primary and secondary woodland. Primary woodland is woodland that has been in existence since the last Ice Age, while secondary woodland, is woodland that has grown up on land that originally had some other use. This secondary woodland may be as old as ancient woodland but is known to have grown up over some former land use. Some secondary woodland may have been planted but much is just old agricultural, grazing or industrial land that has not been kept clear and has reverted to woodland. Although their ecological value is not as great as the ancient woodland they often have great social value and have historical and archaeological significance in terms of change in land use.

Woods that are not ancient are usually known as recent – even though they can have been around for up to 400 years old. So you can have

ancient secondary woodland and recent secondary woodland.

How woodlands work

A woodland is an assemblage of closely planted trees with associations of other plants and animals. They have grown up naturally but may have been extensively managed – particularly in the past.

The typical structure of a woodland in the UK consists of vertical layering or stratification within the vegetation. The upper, canopy layer is

dominated by tall, close growing trees with a more or less continuous canopy. The dominant species give their name to the woodland community – for example oak, beech or Scots Pine woods. Other canopy trees include Ash, birch and Yew. The microclimate they create has a large impact on the species which can survive in their shade.

The first layer in the understory is the shrub layer. Dominated by small trees such as the shade tolerant hazel and holly amongst which the woody climbers clematis and honeysuckle, ivy, dog rose and woody nightshade grow. Just passing through this zone there are also juvenile canopy trees that photosynthesise little but put all their energy into gaining height and reaching into the canopy.

Below the shrub layer is the field layer. In spring these are often dominated by whole fields of bluebells or ransomes. The plants are often clones so they can spread and dominate an area rapidly in their short growing season.

Finally the ground layer lives right on the soil surface, these include the mosses and liverworts. Below ground there is further stratification in the root layer between the roots and micorrhiza of the fungi.

Each layer has its own associated fauna. Most animals have a particular affinity for certain plants so will have their range effectively limited by that plant's position. For example; dormice forage extensively on hazel so are largely found in the shrub layer, Jays and squirrels feed on acorns in the canopy and bees and butterflies largely stick to the field layer. Throughout the woodland layers fungi, mosses and lichens all find their different niches.

Management of woodland trees in the UK historically took the form of coppicing or, on wood pasture, pollarding. Coppicing involves cutting the tree back at its base to encourage the growth of multiple stems which can be cut again and again in rotation and is much more productive that cutting a mature tree just once. Pollarding involves the same process but the tree is cut above head height (2–3m) in areas where the regrowth would be damaged by grazing animals. Most British broadleaf trees will coppice, however conifers do not survive felling, once cut down they do not sprout from the stump or sucker from the roots but will die. Coppice trees that are periodically cut live much longer than uncut trees. The wood from cut coppices is rarely more than arm thick, it is used as fuel and

also to make hurdles and fences. For larger construction some trees must be left to grow to maturity, the larger branches and trunks are required to provide timber for beams and planks. Oak timber has always been prized in this country and oak trees wherever they grew were invariably retained as timber trees.

Man has influenced the smooth running of the woodland by coppicing, felling, introducing grazing animals and generally being a disruptive element. However, coppicing gives a competitive advantage to some shrub and field species which take advantage of the sudden increase in light. In

a coppiced woodland trees, such as hazel or birch, may get a chance to take hold where they would be unable to break from the shrub layer of the unbroken canopy in an uncut woodland. In an unmanaged woodland these trees would get their chance but much less regularly as they would have to wait for canopy trees to succumb to storm damage or disease.

There are an estimated 2 billion people in the world still reliant on wood for cooking and heat (Royal Botanical Gardens, Kew), however, in this country we are no longer dependent on wood for fuel and this has resulted in the lack of

management of many ancient woodlands over the last few decades. The value of woodland management is becoming appreciated again and the number of woodlanders is currently increasing, managing our woodlands in a sustainable manner.

Finding woodlands

When you consider woodland in the UK, the statistics look disappointing: we have just 13 per cent cover compared to a Europe-wide average of around 37 per cent. However the trend is in the right direction as, at the beginning of last century, woodland cover had dropped to an all time low of just 5 per cent (Peterken 1996).

In spite of our bad reputation there are woodlands accessible to all throughout the country, every habitat has woods whether they are coastal, riparian, mountain, heathland or downland. The woods occur as distinct, named woods, sharply defined islands in great seas of farmland, heath or moorland. This means that woods are easy to find and identify whether you are looking on maps, talking to people or searching on the Internet.

Roughly a third of UK woodland is owned and managed by the Forestry Commission, a third by private owners and the other third is split between businesses, charities (including National Trust and Woodland Trust) and local authority and community woodlands. Members of the public have the legal right to access to 90 per cent of Forestry Commission owned woodland and 30 per cent of woodlands owned by other bodies and individuals (Molteno et al 2012).

The best way to find woodlands in any area is to employ a combination of tactics:

Talk to people   People who get out into the countryside regularly for work or pleasure will know the area well – dog walkers, runners and mountain bikers usually cover a lot of ground in an area and can be a good source of information.

Look at the local maps   On Ordnance Survey (OS) maps woodlands are named and coloured green. They all have little tree symbols on them that signify the type of woodland you may expect. Little Christmas trees represent coniferous woodland, mini candyfloss sticks are non-coniferous trees, two long lines by a short squiggle (something like a headless dog) are coppice and the mini candyfloss sticks on a white background are orchard. Not only will the map show you where the woodlands are and some idea of the type of woodland, but you should be able to spot paths, parking, nearby train stations and other activities that may be in the area.

Search the Internet   There are some really good websites that will help you find the nearest accessible woods.

- The Woodland Trust website www. woodlandtrust.org.uk links you through to their Visit Woods website.
- The Forestry Commission website www.forestry.gov.uk has the 'find a forest' facility which allows you to search on woodland names or your town or county.
- The Wildlife Trusts main website, www.wildlifetrust.org, has a search engine for reserves and can also link you through to the local wildlife trust websites which also have search engines for all local reserves.

- The National Trust website, www.nationaltrust.org.uk, allows you to search for local sites which it lists with a description of the property or countryside it contains.

All the websites let you search for sites in your area of interest and then link you through to a page for the sites that it identifies. Along with maps and directions you will find information on the wildlife you may expect to see and any facilities including woodlands trails, sculpture trails, cycle hire, cafes, parking and so on.

Just go for a wander. Heading out in an area to explore on foot, bike, bus or car you will probably spot areas of woodland that you can then either investigate or research using the other tactics mentioned.

According to the Woodland Trust (2010) 63 per cent of us in England and 83 per cent in Scotland have woodland of more than 20Ha within 4km of our homes, so we are never far from the woods. Woodlands provide a great focus for a day out with family and friends not least because of the shelter they afford from the worst vagaries of the British weather. Cool in summer and warm in winter they can provide entertainment and interest for all the family.

Woodland access

In many European states access to woodlands is seen as a fundamental public right, however, the situation is not so straightforward in the UK. The Countryside Rights of Way Act 2000 (CROW) ensured access to the countryside in England and Wales but did not include woodlands in its provisions. It does allow woodland owners to dedicate woodlands as open access land if they wish.

The practicalities of this are that you do not necessarily have legal access to woodlands in the UK. If there is a public right of way in to the wood you can walk through the wood but there is not necessarily legal access off the path, if there is not a foot or bridle path into the woods then there is quite probably no legal access allowed. The Forestry Commission summarises the situation by saying: 'Legally accessible woodland in England and Wales includes the Public Forestry Estate (Forestry Commission owned), NGO owned woodland (e.g. RSPB and National Trust), local authority owned woodland, community woodlands and private woodlands with rights of way or in receipt of woodland improvement grants which have public access as a condition'.

In simple terms, in England and Wales you have legal access anywhere there is a footpath (these are clearly marked on OS maps as orange, green or a fine black dashed line). If the land is open access land you also have legal access off the footpath. Access land is marked on more recent OS maps with a yellow tint which replaces the purple outline on older maps. Woodlands listed on the Woodland Trust and Forestry Commission websites will give you details of the specifics of access at that site. Those with public access will have full access – on and off paths, usually with designated parking areas and information boards.

Scotland has slightly different provisions as the Scottish Land Reform Act 2003 granted a 'right of responsible access' to land and inland water, which includes woodland. This continues the Scottish assumption that the public should have an unhindered access to the countryside and truly have the right to roam. This does not necessarily mean, however, that your presence in all woodland in Scotland is encouraged – just that you have the legal right to be there.

A word on safety

Whenever you go out into the countryside remember you are responsible for your own actions and those of your dependents. Take that responsibility seriously and remember that accidents can happen. It is down to you to use your own judgement and as always when you are considering an activity and the abilities of your dependents. If in doubt, don't. Use your common sense and wield your responsibility wisely but don't let it prevent you from having fun.

It is very easy to get disorientated and lost in

woodland. In general stick together and make sure someone is responsible for navigation.

If you are carrying out activities with young children or in unfamiliar woodland but want to allow some independence it may be wise to have a meeting point of a tree or rock in a clearing. Put or hang a brightly coloured bag or coat at the meeting point and make sure that everyone is the group stays within sight of this at all times to prevent people wandering off and getting lost.

The woods can be a great source of peace and calm in
the midst of a busy existence. Take a gentle stroll, sling a
hammock between two sturdy trees, listen to the birds
and make the most of a spring bluebell carpet.

Relax

Contemplate the canopy

North Downs Way, Colley Hill, Surrey

On a regular dog walk today I passed my favourite, immense beech tree. The tree stands on the lip of an old crater or pit and the roots all along one side are exposed by the steep edge. In contrast to the gnarled fingers of the roots protruding into the murky depths of the dank, leaf filled pit, the smooth trunk of the tree is statuesque and statesman-like; it reaches majestically with its regal posture right up to the clouds. With a girth of around 4m it is probably around 150 years old. Hanging on one of the lower branches is a swing with a branch seat and every time I pass I feel compelled to sit and contemplate the canopy. As I swing out over the void of the pit I lean back and look up through the diminishing branches of the tree. The changing seasons bring different views — I even love to watch shards of rain as they rattle the leaves on their way down to me. From fluorescent green in spring to rich golden brown in autumn and into the bare branches of winter, the view of the canopy is always dizzying, dramatic and aesthetically pleasing. I can't help marvelling at nature's cycles and the constancy of these behemoths that have overseen the activities in these woods for so many years.

How to contemplate the canopy

Lean against a trunk, lie down on the ground, sit on a swing or lie back in a hammock. Whatever you choose, take some time to contemplate the canopy and all that is going on up there.

Like Mina in David Almond's, *Skellig*, be amazed by the abundance of nature. Make a circle of your finger and thumb and look closely at what you see within; a small circle of life. What passes through your small territory as you watch? Focus on the detail. Zoom in on one small area of canopy and investigate it further. Marvel at the density of growth and the leaves. Look at the range of colours and how the trees have devised techniques to capture as much of the sun as possible on their photosynthetic surfaces like finely tuned solar panels. Be amazed at the luxuriance and vitality of life in the treetops.

Try out different trees. The dark green shade of a Yew tree has quite a different feel to the airy froth of a Silver Birch tree and the zinging, lime-green freshness of a springtime beech. Winter skeletons provide little shelter but make for dramatic outlines and it is interesting to see the structure of the tree unwrapped.

Every tree has its own characteristics and their own associated wildlife. Contemplating a canopy in full foliage it can be hard to see the wildlife but sit quietly and you will certainly hear the birds, listen deeper and you may make out the rustlings of smaller creatures about their business too.

Look up into the canopy and
be amazed at the luxuriance
and vitality of life in the
treetops: the variety of the
leaves; the calls of the birds
and rustling of insects.

* Leaves

Hawthorn

As the main food supply to the tree, leaves are extremely important. Ninety per cent of the tree's trunk, branches and root structure comes from carbohydrates produced in the leaves. Using their chlorophyll and water supplied from the roots, leaves can exchange hydrogen from the water with carbon and oxygen from carbon dioxide in the atmosphere to make carbohydrates. This exchange of water from the leaves drives the circulation of sap throughout the tree and can equate to 250 litres an hour in summer (according to the Royal Botanical Gardens Kew), the water from the soil also contains the tree's secondary source of nutrients.

Evergreen leaves are adapted to survive winter, so they have a less efficient evaporation system – thicker skin, a simpler shape, a waxy coat. Deciduous leaves are wide and flat to maximise their photosynthetic potential and are adapted to turn to meet the sunlight flat side on to maximise light absorption. Beech is particularly efficient at this and only allows about five per cent of incident sunlight through to the woodland floor.

WHY SOME TREES LOSE THEIR LEAVES AND OTHERS NOT Some trees have evolved to lose their leaves annually (deciduous) while others have evolved to keep leaf cover throughout the year (evergreen). Individual evergreen leaves still usually last only a year, they just lose them on a rolling programme rather than all at the same time as deciduous trees do.

The main reason these two strategies have evolved is related to productivity. In environments with little seasonal variation, for example in rainforests, growing conditions are good year round, there is no benefit in losing leaves and virtually all the trees are evergreens. In environments with a very dry or cold season with limited sunlight it is better to grow less robust, disposable leaves which are more productive over the growing season. In spite of the high

Birch

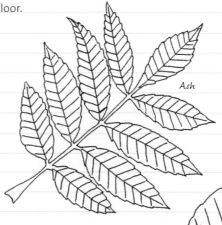

Ash

Beech

Beech

photosynthetic capability of deciduous leaves, their short growing season means that the net photosynthetic gain of a deciduous tree is still lower than the evergreen's over the course of the whole year.

Productivity is not the only factor driving the choice between deciduous and evergreen. The multitude of leaves on a deciduous tree, all heavy with water, can weigh up to several tons in summer. The loss of these water laden leaves in winter releases a huge amount of stress from the branches of deciduous trees and allows them to withstand adverse weather conditions. Evergreens are much more susceptible to damage in winter when snow and ice accumulates on their branches and high winds can cause uprooting and damage to their branches.

Holly

Holly

Oak

Sling a hammock

Majorca ... September

... I have had an epiphany, a realisation, a revelation. I have discovered relaxation! Holidays have always been about new places, discovery, old/new friends, activity and fun but I've never really done relaxation.

This year the kids are three and four and we have rented a finca on a Majorcan hillside. We are in an olive grove grazed by bell wearing sheep, we have an outside kitchen, a small pool and warm weather but best of all we have a couple of hammocks. Heaven. I was born to swing in a hammock. I can stretch out looking up through the silvery olive green shields of the leaves, tracing the lines of the gnarled and twisted branches with the perfect colour contrast of the blue of the sky beyond. The sheep graze around us clanking their harmonious bells and the cicadas thrum out their rhythm all day long providing the perfect soundtrack to the sun beating down and dappling through the cooling leaves of the tree. My daughters climb in soporifically, slightly anaesthetised by hours in the pool and the blanket heat and the thrumming soundtrack and I can read my favourite childhood books to them to my hearts content. This is a holiday.

Back in England and nearly ten years on it is a cold and windy day and I've been hunched over the computer for hours but have achieved little. The broadband is playing up, everything is grinding so slowly I have to wait ten minutes for a two line email to go. I have switched on and off, reset the home hub but nothing changes. In desperation I phone the helpline, a list of options as long as my arm – 'so they can direct me to someone who can help as quickly as possible'. Clearly technical problems are not as high a priority as sales and I am on hold for 20 minutes – still listening to musak and intermittent reassurances that my call is very important to them and I should keep holding. I have half an hour before I need to collect the girls from school, do I continue with my fruitless quest? No, I put my hammock on my back and head to the wood at the back of the park. Twenty metres off the main track I find a couple of ideal trees and sling my hammock. I swing myself in at shoulder height and lie back. I am swinging gently, the winter sun is just peeking out between clouds and cuts through the bare trunks of trees angling towards my refuge. The bare branches of the tree make dramatic silhouettes against the grey sky. Squirrels chase across my field of vision chattering aggressively to one another. I can hear jays and crows high in the trees around me. My shoulders, in layers of jumpers and coat begin to relax. Who needs technology when this is calling? ...

Tips for hammocks

The Book of Idle Pleasures extols the virtues of lying in a hammock and describes the art of finding 'hammockable' trees. Hammockable trees need to be about two and half metres apart and strong enough to stand up to the sideways pull of you hammock. Anything that you struggle to get both hands round or bigger should be sufficient. Depending on your hammock and your technique for hanging it, you probably also need a branch, or at least substantial a nobble, on each tree which can be a challenge. Coppiced woodlands are not ideal places to look for hammockable trees as there is so much upward growth but little of it is thick enough to support a hammock and there are very few lateral branches. Woodlands with a few more timber trees are a better bet for finding suitable slinging places.

Following that Majorcan holiday I have become something of a hammock connoisseur. My first purchase was a micro hammock: made of parachute material it packs into a bag the size of a Cornish pasty and goes on holiday with us everywhere. We also now have a mega, double canvas hammock for extended use in the garden (along with several smaller canvas and string hammocks as the family has grown), we have a hammock chair in our kitchen and – a recent addition – a highly technical tree hammock for use in woodland expeditions. This one has webbing straps that you sling twice round the tree, the hammock is then slung completely flat

between the trees and the tension is sufficient to hold the hammock up without needing side branches. This makes the whole process much easier. We are now fully hammocked up and I would urge you to consider a hammock.

Once you have slung your hammock all your cares can drift away and you can just be. Let your thoughts wander, contemplate the canopy and waste some time.

Wasting time is an interesting phenomenon. In my philosophy wasting time properly is never a waste of time. Wasting time is when you are aiming to achieve something but faffing around and failing to achieve anything. Wasting time properly; as in sitting and staring into space, peering off a bridge, daydreaming and lying in a hammock – this kind of wasting time is never a waste of time. All kinds of revelations and inspirations come to us in these moments. Surely Newton was wasting time sitting around under a tree when he discovered gravity. So go on, waste some time, you never know where it may get you.

Hug a tree

Tree hugging developed a bad press when environmentalists were derogatorily referred to as 'treehuggers'. It was particularly aimed at environmental activists who used a tactic of non- violent direct action in the 1990's. Typical action would involve chaining themselves to trees and campin g in treehouses to try to prevent developments which threatened to destroy woodlands in their path. A particularly memorable occasion was when the campaigner known as Swampy, moved into tunnels in a woodland and his comrades chained themselves to trees to prevent the development of the A30's Honiton Bypass.

In the spirit of the 1980s campaign where

parents were urged to hug their child, I am on a mission to bring back tree hugging. Hugging a tree is not a just a way to demonstrate your love for the tree. A hug will tell you many things about the tree you are hugging.

How to age a tree

Every year a tree adds a new layer of sapwood to its trunk so with every year it gets a bit fatter. Different trees grow at different rates, so if you know what type of tree you are hugging you can estimate its age. By stretching your arms around the girth of a tree at its waist (narrowest point) you can estimate the age of the tree using the table opposite.

NAME OF TREE	DIVIDE GIRTH (CM) BY THIS NUMBER
Oak	2
Hazel, Elm, Ash, Beech	2.5
Holly, Yew	1.25
Pine, Spruce	3.25
Sycamore	2.75

For the average person your arm span will measure the same as your height. So by hugging a tree – either on your own or with some friends you can make a rough calculation of the tree's girth. If you want to be more accurate you can take a tape measure but it is not as fun.

This beech tree in Wilderness Woods is a perfect example. Poppy and Thea are both 1.5m

tall and Lottie is 1.25m so their combined arms spans are 4.25m. Divided by 2.5 this gives a rough age of 170 years.

The tree hugging game

In the tree hugging game the aim is to try to identify an individual tree by giving it a good hug. The player is blindfolded in an area with a few trees. Spin the player around gently and then lead them to a tree. They should then hug the tree, smell it, feel the bark with their hands and generally investigate it for a minute or so. Lead them away from their tree, spin them around again and then remove the blindfold.

Their challenge is to see if they can identify which tree they hugged by remembering how big it was, what the texture of the bark felt like, how it smelt and any other clues they picked up.

* The structure of a tree trunk

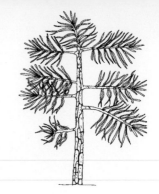

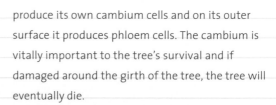

Trees are classified on the basis of their strong woody stem or trunk which differentiates them from other plants. Working from the outside in there are five layers that make up the tree trunk.

The bark is a rough, protective outer layer produced by its own specialised cambium throughout the year; the position of this cambium dictates the form the bark takes.

The inner bark layer is called the phloem. Its job is to transport carbohydrate rich sap from the leaves down to the roots to nourish them and allow for their growth and development. This sap can be tapped to make sugar rich drinks.

Just inside the bark is a single cell thick layer called the cambium. The cambium is the only part of the tree able to produce new wood and can create three types of cell at one time.

On its inner surface it creates new xylem cells to repopulate the sapwood. As it does this, to keep up with the expansion of the trunk, it must produce its own cambium cells and on its outer surface it produces phloem cells. The cambium is vitally important to the tree's survival and if damaged around the girth of the tree, the tree will eventually die.

The sapwood, or xylem, is formed of long thin cells in broadleaved trees and its structure allows the miracle of the transport of water up into the leaves of the trees. Throughout the growing season there is a continuous column of water passing up a tree from its roots into its leaves. This may be a height of 300ft. Imagine sitting at the top of a tree with a 300ft straw and trying to suck water out of a glass while sitting on the ground. The tree uses the amazing property of water tension and the very long thin cells of the sapwood to enable this process to take place. Once the leaves start photosynthesising they exert a pressure on the water to draw it up through the tree. In spring the roots also exert a pressure to start the sap rising and this column of water is then maintained throughout the spring and summer.

As the cambium produces new sapwood each growing season the old sapwood lignifies and hardens to join the heartwood of the tree. The heartwood is dead wood which forms the rigid backbone of the tree. As long as the tree remains intact the heartwood will retain its integrity but as soon as there is any damage and air gets through the outer casing of the tree the heartwood decays and rots away.

TREE RINGS AND WHAT THEY TELL US: THE STUDY OF DENDROCHRONOLOGY When we look at the surface of a felled tree we can see rings of light and dark wood. The rapid spring growth requires large quantities of sap and wider cells resulting in a pale ring. In summer the growth rate is slower and the smaller cells produce the darker circle in the sapwood. By counting the number of dark rings we can establish the age of the felled tree.

The Ancient Greeks understood that you could look at a tree's growth rings to determine its age but it was only in 1901 that an astronomer (A.E. Douglass) at the Arizona Lowell Observatory had the idea to cross-match the ring sizes with meteorological data. He discovered that the width of the spring and summer growth is directly correlated to the rain and sun conditions at the time the ring is being laid down. Growth rings, particularly those from temperate trees at the edge of their environmental tolerance, therefore, are a prefect record for weather conditions throughout the life of the tree

Dendrochonologists have expanded on Douglass's early work and looking at ring data from ancient tree remains including the European Oak it has been possible to create a continuous series of rings and hence interpolate meteorological data back 10,000 years (to the last ice age) on every continent other than Antarctica.

It is not just the weather records that are of interest. In the 1970s Hans Suess used tree rings to calibrate carbon 14 radio dating techniques. Initial results showed that carbon 14 dating assumptions of constant levels of carbon in the atmosphere were not correct and lead to alterations in the dating of many ancient artefacts. The implications of this work in many fields of science were huge (Bernd Kromer 2009).

Bewilderwood, Norfolk ... December

... We went to Bewilderwood today. A proper cold winter's day but in-spite of the cold we stayed for hours at this magical, wild adventure park. After a couple of hours investigating the mini tree houses and high level walkways, swings and mazes we stopped for steaming jacket potatoes. By the picnic benches they had a huge bonfire burning. Beside the fire they were handing out pinecones and pieces of paper. Everyone was encouraged to write down their wishes and dreams on a piece of paper, fold it over and tuck it between the scales of the cone. These were then thrown into the fire where they could be heard crackling and popping. Once burned the dreams and wishes were supposed to go up in smoke and hopefully come true. We loved this and spent some time coming up with lots of ideas so that we could stay warm by the fire and watch our dreams being engulfed in flames ...

How to make a woodland message

There are lots of ways that messages can be presented using woodland resources. One year my friend's sister was working in Japan and sent a beautiful autumnal Japanese maple leaf with a message written on it in metallic pen. It looked absolutely beautiful. You could collect some pretty leaves in autumn and write on memories, dreams, poems or birthday wishes. These could then be hung on a branch in a vase or stuck onto a card or even framed as a picture

I have recently been collecting shards of fallen bark – cherry, silver birch, eucalyptus, plane trees and yew trees all have beautiful bark which you will find shreds of shed beneath the tree. Go out after a period of dry weather and collect some. The inside of the bark is very smooth. I particularly like the small scales that flake off the yew tree. The inside surface is as smooth as velvet and has wonderful patterns on it that look like a polished wood grain. I draw on these with a black ink pen and they make a great alternative to a birthday card. Or, boxed up, it can make an unusual present.

Or when back at home, why not make your own small fire. Collect some pinecones, write out your wishes and dreams and send them up to the heavens in smoke.

Collect shards of fallen bark. You'll find that the inner surface is as smooth as velvet to the touch and beautifully patterned like polished wood.

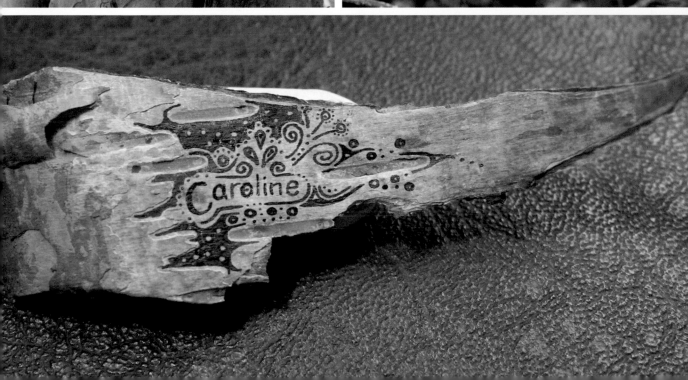

Caroline

Go in search of woodland spirits

Norwich Cathedral, Norfolk ... August

... There is nothing better than a bit of nostalgia and going back to your roots. If you can take good friends and show them something of your heritage it is somehow even better. On a wet rainy day in Norfolk last summer I took some good friends to Norwich Cathedral. Norwich Cathedral has been standing as long as many or our ancient trees. Built between the Norman invasion of 1066 and the signing of the Magna Carta in 1215, its immense vaulted architecture has always enthralled me. Many is the service where I tipped back my head and gazed at the web of stonework with its constellation of medieval stone bosses. To save visitors cricking their necks the cathedral supplies some fantastic mirrored trolleys. Basically a wheeled wooden table, the tops are a big, slightly angled mirror so that by looking down you can see the bosses reflected. With the ten children between us it took me right back to my childhood and the temptation to whizz up and down the aisles standing on the trolley bar. We did manage to restrain the urge and spent some considerable time searching the bosses for the bible stories but also some more unexpected images. One of these was the 'green man'. The green man is quite a common image in many churches throughout the country and is a reminder of the significance of natural imagery and perhaps our pagan past ...

Woodland spirits

The green man is a mysterious spirit. He is at times a benevolent force and at other times seems to be quite terrifyingly wild, erupting into lush growths from mouth, nose ears and eyes. His image can be seen all over this country, very often in surprising numbers in churches. The green man has been linked with Pan or Herne the god of nature. He epitomises the life force of the woodland, the circle of life, the renewal and rebirth of nature. Dying back in winter to burst forth with new vigour in spring. The god of the greenwood he is the symbol of rebirth and a precursor to the story of the Messiah. It is a cyclical growth, cutting back and re-growing throughout the cycle of the year. The same story is retold in folk tales including Jack in the Green, John Barleycorn and the Oak King and may be the basis of the legendary Robin Hood. They are all stories along a theme.

If you want to find images of the green man, *The Green Man in Britain* by Fran and Geoff Doell is a lovely book that investigates his many dimensions and includes a gazetteer of 200 sites including 1000 carvings that can be seen throughout Britain. Alternatively *Countryfile* magazine has a Google maps site of 'Green Man Locations UK' and although not exhaustive it has a good starting collection of sites to visit.

The dryads are another kind of tree spirit. Like the trees themselves they are ancient and venerable beings. If you are able to sit in their green and dappled shade they exude steady strength and give courage to those in need. Even small saplings can have great strength drawing on their combined consciousness of the massed trees in the woodland.

Dryads are typically perceived as humanlike although generally much taller and very ancient. Gathered together into a sacred grove or woodland they form a natural cathedral, both physically and, in pagan rituals, spiritually. It is the essence of these images of dryads that have been used extensively in literature and are called upon by Tolkien as the Ents to support the forces of good in *The Lord of the Rings*.

✳ Trees and their folklore

Virtually all our native trees have some ancient folklore and mythology associated with them. In pagan beliefs trees and their fruits could be used to either repel the spirits and faeries or used to call on them for their help where needed.

YEW The most ancient of all our native trees, the yew can live several thousand years. In Norbury, Surrey, there are ancient groves of yew that are believed to be druid groves. Given their longevity these trees may actually have been around when the druids still ruled as the high priests of the Celtic tribes up to around 2000 BC.

The Yew tree symbolised death and resurrection in Celtic times. This may be due to their poisonous needles and ability to root where their drooping branches touch the ground. Even in later Christian times their boughs were still buried with the dead.

OAK The druids revered the oak as the most powerful and significant of the trees. The druid name is believed to mean 'oak knowledge' coming either from the Greek *drys* for oak or from the Gaelic *duir* meaning oak.

Throughout the UK there are a number of ancient oak trees that are known as Gospel oaks.

In early Christian times these oak trees were used as an open-air pulpit before a church building was available. John Wesley – founder of the Methodist church – was particularly well known for preaching under gospel trees as he built up his following and before he established a network of Methodist chapels.

ASH The Ash has always been a magical, mystical wood considered to be protective and healing. People would put ash around their houses to ward off evil magic and the little people. Newborn babies were often given a spoonful of ash sap to make them strong. The Greek nature deities were nymphs of the Ash tree.

ROWAN In Greek mythology the Rowan tree was formed when the goddess of youth, Hebe, lost the cup of ambrosia she was carrying to the gods. An eagle was sent to recover it and, while fighting the demons for the cup, it shed feathers and blood that formed the leaves and berries of the rowan tree where they reached the earth.

The tree has long been seen as the tree of vision and protection. This may be due to the fact that the berries have a five-sided star or pentagram, a symbol of protection, on the opposite side to the stalk. The twigs were often hung inside doorways while people hung them around their own and their cattle's necks as protection against witchcraft. The druids burnt rowan to raise the force of warriors for protection and to call forth prophetic visions.

HAWTHORN Known as the May tree because it blossoms in May, faeries were believed to live around solitary hawthorn trees which were seen as the entrance to the Celtic underworld.

It is extensively used in May Day celebrations and as the goddess tree, the May Queen would often wear a crown of Hawthorn on 1 May when she wed the young hunter god. May twigs would often be collected and used in decorations outside the home for the May celebration but never inside the house. The Hawthorn was seen as very unlucky and bringing it in the house could cause illness and even death in the family. It is believed the link with death is related to the blossom, said to resemble the smell of death. Later investigations found that the blossom emits trimethylamine that is also released by decaying animal tissue.

ELDER The Elder is another protective wood and is the home of the ancient and wise Elder mother. She will grant access to the faery world and heal a weary soul. If you sleep beneath the branches you will be taken to the faeries.

MISTLETOE Druids, as you may know from the delightful fictional druid, Getafix in the *Asterix* books, used mistletoe extensively in their potions. When growing on apple, or even better oak, trees it was seen as the seed of the sky god and was the primary power plant of the Celts.

These days, faeries are seen as playful creatures and children love stories of faeries and the little folk. Near us we have a tree in which someone has created a tiny door. It is a great focus on walks to see the little offerings left for the faeries along with miniature letters.

Listen to the birds

Four Sticks Wood, Norfolk ... May

... I've had a few days of monk-like existence writing with no other distractions at my Granny's old house in Norfolk. Tucked away behind tangled hedges and set in the middle of its own land I am cut off from the daily comings and goings of my own life and everyone else's. As I sit at the table in the living room window there is no need to close the curtains as dusk falls, there is no one to see in; but as I sit typing I am distracted by a white shadow silently passing by. This becomes a regular occurrence as I tap away and peer pensively out into the deepening gloom. As the dark creeps up, my nightly visitor passes by without a whisper but turns and looks through the window at me, solemnly wishing me 'good evening' as he passes on to his night's hunting. Barn owls are probably the most beautiful of birds. Their ghostly whiteness and silent flight lend them a surreal almost supernatural air. They come and go with no fanfare or drama, their appearance is always a treat; like an unexpected gift received, a sign from beyond that all is well ...

How to listen to the birds

Birds can be hard to see in woodlands, particularly when the trees are fully dressed in their summer foliage and we rarely catch more than a glimpse of them as they pop in and out of the canopy. However, even when out of sight birds are clearly in evidence in the woods and can be heard singing and scuffling around at all times of year. While we may hear their birdsong it is very easy to gloss over it and miss out on listening to the calls and songs in an attempt to decipher the individual calls of the birds.

Walk through or sit in the woods at springtime and you will be assaulted by a cacophony of noise as territories and partners are vied and fought for. Identifying the different species when they are largely invisible is an art. Some calls are distinctive and immediately recognisable; many of us will be able to distinguish the cawing of the

Robn

Walk through the woods in springtime and you will be assaulted by a cacaphony of noise from birds finding a mate, breeding and calling to their young.

Chaffinch

Pied Flycatcher

Nuthatch

crows, the raucous *kaaaa* of the Jay and the *yaffle* of the Green Woodpecker. The Great Spotted Woodpecker doesn't have the *yaffle* but can be heard knocking on the trees to locate his territory in spring. At night pairs of Tawny Owls make the *t'wit* and responding *t'woo* hoot; these and are the most likely of our native owls to be heard in woodland. Also at night in spring and summer, on the edge of woodland you may hear the two-tone *churr* of the Nightjar along with their distinctive wing clap as they appear to applaud themselves.

How to learn to identify birdsong

Less easy to distinguish are the calls of the 'little brown jobs' (lbj's), the many small birds that often flit around the margins of woods feeding and roosting. If you can find someone who knows bird-song I would urge you to capture them and force them to accompany to the woodland to help you identify the songs – make them keep doing it until you have also learnt to identify the songs. A whole new world is opened up to you if you are with someone who can actually identify which bird is singing and if you can learn those skills yourself it is like having a Babel fish (that brilliant instant translator from *The Hitch Hiker's Guide to the Galaxy*) inserted in your ear.

If you don't have an accommodating friend or acquaintance with the right skills, the National Trust, Local Wildlife Trusts and local birding groups often organise walks and rambles in the woods where you can go along with an expert who will help you to identify birdsong. Have a look at your nearest National Trust visitor centre, RSPB centre and in local libraries and parks as well as in magazines and online to find out activities that are organised in your area.

Other useful resources, if you prefer the DIY approach, are available in the form of CDs available from a number of sources. Online, the RSPB website has birdsong along with each bird page and smartphones have some great apps which you can download which allow you to record a birdsong as well as playing the birdsongs of individual birds. Ebook field guides are increasingly available that allow you to hear a bird's call as well as making a visual identification.

My approach to learning birdsong is two pronged. While out on my walk, I will listen out for a very distinctive bird song being sung close by. When I have isolated the song I stalk the sound until I have found the tree the song is coming from and eventually narrow down the location until I can hopefully identify the bird in question. If I don't recognise the bird I will stop and listen and watch carefully, doing my very best to imprint the song and the bird's appearance in my mind. Back at home I will use all resources available, books, smartphone apps and websites to try to identify bird and song and then on subsequent walks I will try to tease out the new song from the choir of birds around me.

Alternatively I will plan my search before I go out. I will decide that today is the day I really nail the chaffinch song and I will listen to their song on websites and apps until I think I can identify it and then go out in search.

In some cases people have tried to pick out the more distinctive songs and 'translated' them into phrases to try to help us identify which bird is which. For example: 'a little bit of bread and no cheeese' is the phrase associated with the

Yellowhammer song, you may recognise this because it was popularised by Enid Blyton in her children's books.

There is also:

> *take two turns, Taffy* – Woodpigeon
> *united, united, united* – Collared Dove
> *tree, tree, tree, once more I come to thee* –
>   Pied Flycatcher

If you listen out for a new song see if you can fit a phrase to it to help you identify when the same bird is singing another time.

My own versions that I used to help me learn the Blue Tit and Great Tit are:
Take two. Take two. for the Great Tit which is very vocal and easily identified.
The Blue Tit has a warbly variation on this which is *take take, two-o-o-o* with a warble on the two.

Blue Tit

Yellowhammer

Barn Owl

* Tawny Owl (Strix aluco)

Mysterious, rarely-seen birds of the night, flying silently on the wing, scanning the woodland with their large eyes, owls have an air of authority that has given them their reputation for wisdom and their mythical role as messengers and consorts of witchcraft. In Greek mythology, Athena the goddess of wisdom is often shown holding an owl, while to the ancient Romans an owl's hoot was seen as a harbinger of death.

Owls have a strong presence in art and culture: from correcting Winnie the Pooh, carrying Harry Potter's messages, assisting Merlin and sailing away for a year and a day with a pussy cat they have a strong literary presence. These days the owl adorns every piece of stationary and household decoration you can imagine.

The owl you are most likely to see and hear in British broadleaf woodland is the Tawny Owl, the most common and wide spread of British owls. The female and male owl both make the distinctive rising *kee-wick* call while only the male has the easily reproduced *to-whoo*. The two calls together make the classic *to-whit-to-whoo* call that you will often hear at night near woodlands.

Tawny Owls pair off and remain in their monogamous pairing. They usually nest in a tree hole where the female incubates their clutch of two to three eggs and the male feeds the young. They are highly territorial and non-migratory and young can sometimes find it hard to establish a territory when they are forced out of the nest and may perish.

Tawny Owls feed nocturnally and have asymmetrically placed ears to help them when hunting. Once they have located their prey they drop from a favourite perch onto the small mammals and rodents that they eat whole, regurgitating the indigestible bits in grey pellets.

As with all owls, their flight is almost silent by virtue of their soft upper feathers and fringed front edge to their outer primaries. The Tawny has shorter, rounder wings than many of the other species, allowing it to manoeuvre in small spaces amongst the trees.

The Little Owl and Long-eared Owl also live in woodlands but usually in different places to the Tawny Owl as they are unable to compete with the stronger Tawny which may sometimes even take them as prey.

Long-eared Owl

Little Owl

Tawny Owl

* Jay (Garrulus glandarius)

The colourful squirrel of the crow family is also probably the least visible. Living in woodlands it is most often seen swooping from one tree to another exposing its blue wing flash and distinctive white rump while emitting a harsh shriek. When alarmed Jays can raise their crest feathers, which can give a momentary impression of a Hoopoe.

The Celtic name, *schreachag choille* – screamer of the woods – sums up the Jay's character perfectly. They are highly intelligent members of the crow family and possibly as a result of their shy nature and secretive ways they appear very rarely in folklore or literature. However, if attacked by a hawk or owl, a Jay will mob the bird of prey, mimicking the cry of its attacker as it does so.

They are most active in autumn when they search for acorns, beech mast and hazelnuts which they often bury or hide in nooks and crannies for retrieval in winter. In addition to nuts and seeds they eat insects, eggs, nestlings and small mammals. Jays may store several thousand acorns in a season and are important birds for the spread of oak woodlands. A Jay can fit nine acorns in its crop as it flies off to find a good burial site within its territory.

The male and female usually pair for life and build untidy twig nests together in trees and shrubs. The female will incubate the four to six eggs on the nest while the male brings her food, and they both feed the young once they hatch. Unmated individuals gather together in large numbers in March to find their life partners in what are known as 'crow marriages'.

There have been occasional invasions of large numbers of Jays from Europe when the acorn harvest has failed. Thousands were recorded in several places along the UK's southern and eastern coastlines, most recently in autumn 1983 and in smaller numbers in autumn 1993 (*www.birdsofbritain.co.uk*).

Feed your senses

Old Simms Copse, North Downs ... May

... I have been walking around for weeks now anticipating the arrival of the bluebells. One of the sure signs that spring has finally sprung is the arrival of the purple-blue haze that spreads through the woodland undergrowth. I have stalked the spiky green shoots which have shown no sign of progressing until, a few days ago, I discovered a few spots of colour that has suddenly turned into a full on purple rash. Now everywhere I turn, I am surrounded by woodlands sporting their purple carpets. Every spring requires a visit to one of the best displays in the area, an ancient, undisturbed woodland high on the North Downs known as Old Simms Copse. We reach the Surrey Wildlife Trust car park only to find that Lottie is fast asleep. Strapping her into a backpack, we head into the woods to take in the dense purple colour, a loud announcement that spring has arrived.

The older girls run around the labyrinth of tamped earth paths, their eyes like saucers, heads on swivels and mouths stuck in perpetual O's. The density of the beautiful flowers compels you to stick to the paths for fear of crushing them. The individual points of colour in the foreground merges to an opacity that then fades like an ocean to the horizon in all directions; we could not tear our eyes away. It was only when we returned to the car that we realised one member of the family had missed the whole spectacle. Lottie was still fast asleep ...

How to feed your senses

To get the most out of a woodland visit you should try to engage all your senses. It is easy to look around you to take in the colours and textures and if you are not making too much of your own noise you will probably hear a few sounds but how much of the detail you take in is another matter. The woodland is also full of great smells, textures and tastes that deserve some of your attention.

Challenge yourself to spend five minutes focusing on each sense. You may need to close your eyes or cover your ears so you don't get too distracted and to help you really focus.

Sight With the short horizon available in the woods it is easy to focus on details close by. There is so much to see. Think like and artist and observe the minute details of your surroundings. Look from a distance and then get right up close to take in the details of the colours, shapes and structures on display. At the widest scale every season is a changing colour-scape with the spring flowers of bluebell, garlic and anemone, bright

green mosses at the base of trees, and the often muted palette of the Farrow and Ball lichens. The tree leaves themselves provide a wide range of colours from the bright spring lime greens to the vibrant oranges, yellow and reds of autumn. Snow in a birch wood presents a monochrome world of intense contrasts where the form and function of the tree's skeleton stands out bold and dramatic. Bird life flits by providing sudden moments of movement and contrast and in autumn mushrooms emerge unannounced their moist surfaces and unearthly shapes and colours looking as though they would be more at home in a rock pool than a woodland.

Hearing Close your eyes and listen to the sounds around you. Listen to the wind in the leaves and branches and small animals scuttling past: a squirrel barking in anger, Jays and other crows raucously shrieking; finches and tits arguing over territory. The soap opera of the canopy can pass us by as we walk below but sit and listen and it's all there going on above you. Listen to your footsteps on the ground, leaf litter, gravel, rock or mud. Put your ear right up to the bark of a tree and you can almost hear the gnawing of a wood-eating beetle.

Bluebells

Bluebells are probably the best known and best loved of all the woodland flowers. Ben Law, woodman of Prickly Nut Wood and an early participant in Grand Designs, was once told by a colour therapist that the colour combinations of bluebells against brown bark and vibrant new leaf growth is one of the calmest combinations of colour you can get. There is certainly something very tranquil about a walk in the cool of an ancient woodland in full bluebell glory. An element of that feeling of calm may come from the soporific scent of the bluebell but don't be lulled into a false sense of security because Endymion the bluebells original familial name (before taxonomists renamed it Hyacinthoides) comes from the Greek son of Zeus. The moon fell in love with him and kissed his eyes as he was sleeping, committing him to a dreamless sleep forever. Bluebells are just one of the many poisonous woodland plants you may encounter so don't be tempted to sample them.

animals presence. Ask some one to lead you blindfolded as you breath in the scents or walk yourself but stop every few minutes, close your eyes and breath in the scent deeply for a minute or two and see what you can distinguish and how it changes.

Touch With your eyes closed try the hug a tree game from the chapter above. Feel the different textures of the woodland: the deeply crenellated chasms of the oak tree; the smooth, elephantine skin of the beech and the shiny, lined paper bark of the birch. Every tree has a very different bark pattern: develop your sense of touch and you may find you can identify the species from the feel of the bark alone – stun and amaze your friends with this as a party trick. Try taking your shoes off and feel the ground textures between your toes. The deep silent needles of a pine wood can feel soft, search out the exposed roots of the trees and wriggle your toes along them to feel their knots and knobbles. Lower your foot onto a bed of moss – Scholl sandals can't beat that for a refreshing foot massage.

Smell Eyes and ears disabled you can give your nose a chance to do some work. All trees have their own distinct smell. Breathe deeply through your nose and you can instantly distinguish pine woodland, from deciduous woodland, from a larch wood. Pine smells most when cut or on a hot day while the birch smells best when wet, it has an almost alcoholic density to its odour after rain. Seasonal plants, fungi and flowers all give their own scent. Bluebells have a harsh smell while wild garlic is instantly recognisable, the fungal mustiness of autumn and damp leaf litter are all evocative of the woodland. Even the animals of the woods leave their smell, stop by a Badger sett or a Fox's hole – you can smell the

Taste Taste is a little trickier, make sure you know which of the plants are poisonous and which not. Once you are confident try grazing a few leaves. Chris Holland (2012) suggests you literally walk around the wood hands behind your back and graze on the soft young leaves of trees (oak, Beech, Hawthorn, lime and pine are all fine while young), garlic and dead nettle. If you are uncertain of your plant identification, why not take your own picnic and eat that wearing a blindfold – all the tastes will seem quite different.

* Woodland flowers

Snowdrops

The blue haze of spring is very distinctive in this country but bluebells are not the only flowers that have managed to adapt to the low light levels prevalent under the woodland canopy. Flowering plants in woodlands have usually adopted one of three strategies to enable them to make the most of the limited light.

SEED-BANK PLANTS, such as the foxgloves are opportunistic species that will lie dormant for many seasons before they get their chance in the sunlight. Their seeds lie in wait in the leaf litter until a branch or whole tree falls, or is felled, at which point they respond to the increase in light and burst into flower. These plants are particularly well adapted to the coppice cycle in ancient managed woodlands. They flourish as the coppice cycle reaches their part of the woodland filling the cleared cant with their colour and vibrancy and then retreating again as the trees grow up.

SPRING LEAFING PERENNIALS are the vernal or pre-vernal flowers, such as the primrose, bluebell, violet and anemone. Every year these flowers respond to that short season in the woods when the levels of sunlight increase in early spring, before the trees fully clothe themselves and relegate the undergrowth to shade for the next six months. These are the flowers we most associate with woodlands and bring on their colour display each year. Most well known of these are the bluebells and the wild garlic (ransoms) that create the carpet of colour. The link between ancient woodlands and spring leafing perennials is very strong and these are particularly characteristic woodland flowers. By leafing and flowering early in spring they get ten times more light than the summer leafers manage later in the year.

SUMMER LEAFING PERENNIALS such as woodruff and dogs mercury are the few woodland plants that are well adapted to low light levels and manage to gather enough light under the canopy to struggle on as summer leafing perennials.

Sweet Violet

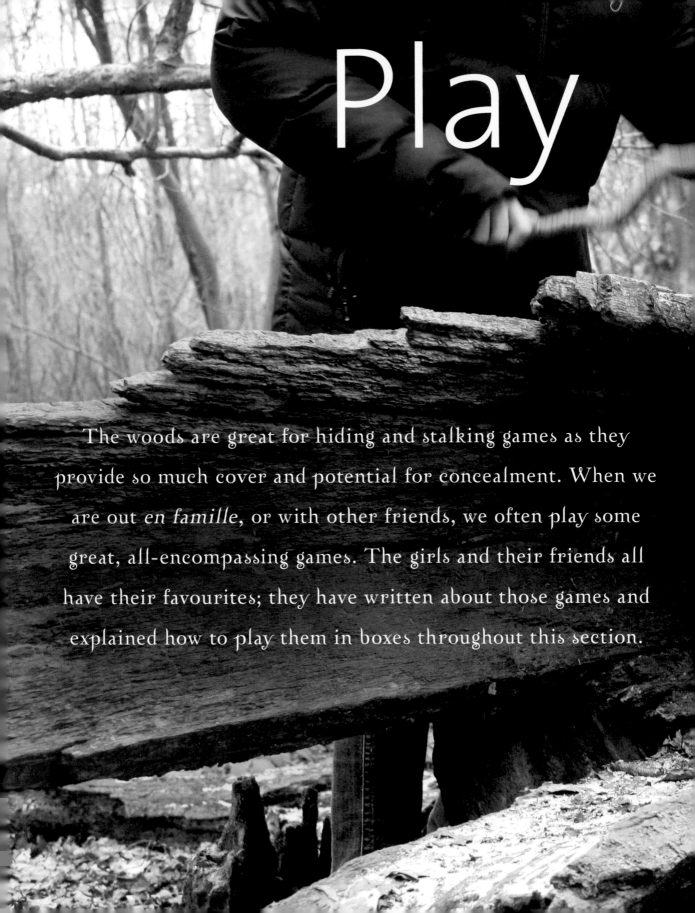

Play

The woods are great for hiding and stalking games as they provide so much cover and potential for concealment. When we are out *en famille*, or with other friends, we often play some great, all-encompassing games. The girls and their friends all have their favourites; they have written about those games and explained how to play them in boxes throughout this section.

Hide and seek is good to play in the woods. It is easy to find a hiding spot like behind trees, in bushes, under leaves or even up a tree. But there's loads more ...

When you are playing you'll need three things:
1. Yourself
2. Friends
3. Somewhere to hide (a wood is perfect)

If you are a hider there are three steps:
1. Think of a hiding place
2. Find it
3. Get in it

If you are a seeker, there are two steps:
1. Count to 30
2. Find your friends!

The last hider to be found is the winner.

I find hide and seek really fun in the woods because it is easy to slip away to another hiding spot. Also I love exploring while I'm looking for my friends. Sometimes I see insects scuttling on the muddy floor or birds flying overhead. When I hide I like to talk to the woodpeckers, I trick my friends by finding a good stick and banging it on a hollow tree – sometimes a woodpecker answers back, it's good fun! My favourite thing when I am a seeker is when my dog Alfie just finds my friends for me. He! He!

Once, me and my family were on a boring walk so my sisters hid in front. When we couldn't find them we shouted 'squeak piggy squeak!' So they squeaked and we could find them. Yay!

Lottie Wardley age 7

Scavenging

Park Hill Woods, Reigate

... Some of my happiest days have been spent pottering around in a wood with small children. My friend Claire and I would pick up our girls from their morning of playgroup and head off across the park and up into the wood. The girls would soon start spotting treasures that they wanted to keep, making up stories and devising fiendish adventures. Claire, with little Laila strapped to her front, would always have a good supply of bags so that the bigger girls could collect all the delights they found. By the end of our walk we would have a huge assortment of natural treats including spiky beech masts, pinecones, feathers, sticks of all shapes and sizes, seed helicopters, and autumn leaves of every colour, shape and size ...

How to scavenge in the woods

Many hours of fun can be spent in the woods with a curious child. There are always things to look at and investigate if you take the time to travel slowly. The speed of a small child is perfect and they are not constrained by our adult desire to get somewhere or achieve a goal. So much of what we stride on by is worthy of further investigation (although I'm not sure how much of it really needs to come back into my house, by the bagful, week after week after week after week).

You don't really need a plan for scavenging in woodland. With small children just take it slow and look down and up and all around. Be curious and think about where everything has come from and what it could be – if you look around you, you can probably work out where it came from and fit it into your surroundings.

If you find you need more incentive to your search; or you would rather limit its scope, see if you can find treasures that meet certain criteria. Maybe you could consider making a picture with what you find. So if you are aiming to make a picture of a monster for example you would try to find materials that would help: feathers and leaves for coats, wings or limbs; acorns, beech nuts or stones as eyes and ears; sycamore helicopters as eyebrows or legs. Let your imagination run wild.

Set yourselves a challenge. Collect as many things beginning with a single letter or of a particular texture or colour. Stick to a theme and collect as many different feathers or as many different shapes of leaf or different shapes and sizes of pinecones or bits of textured bark as you can. Collect fairy related items – a beech mast shell as a spiky hat, acorn cups as crockery, a sycamore helicopter as a boomerang. There are so many bits and pieces in the woods there should be no limits to your scavenging.

Remember scavenging means collecting things that have fallen to the ground, not picking them from the living plants and animals.

You don't really need a
plan when you are
scavenging in woodland.
Just take it slow: the speed
of a small child is the
perfect pace.

Capture the flag is a game of strategy and warfare.

This game is best played with at least six players split into two teams. The more people playing, the better the game usually is.

First, you find a big area of land that can be divided into two territories. Make sure you have a rough boundary of where you are playing and a clear line down the middle dividing up the two territories. A path or a small stream makes an ideal dividing line. Each group then choses a brightly coloured flag — usually a jumper, waterproof or bag which they hang somewhere visible near the back of their territory. Then each team decides on the part of their land which is going to be the prison — this is usually some way from the flag in the middle of their 'land'. We find it is most fun if it is not too far from the boundary line.

The aim of the game is to capture the other team's flag and bring it back to your own territory. But it isn't that easy, there are some rules:

When you are in your opponents' territory they can capture you and put you in their prison. You are safe from capture in your own land. You can only get out of the prison if one of your teammates frees you by tapping you. You then have to return to your own land before you can rejoin the game.

The first team to get both flags over to their side is the winner.

There are lots of cunning tactics you can use in this game. Some examples are:
• The attack and defence tactic: half of your team is defending the flag, while the other half is attacking the other side.
• The dummy tactic: two attackers act as dummies and run straight through the middle of the land, while the players on the other team are distracted, two other players go around the side and get the flag.
• The sprint tactic: everyone on your team apart from one or two defence players will make a sprint for the flag, leaving the opposition confused.

The game can last for ages and we often have to call a temporary truce to have some food but it is great fun — and exhausting! Good luck!

Thea Wardley age 12

Conkers, I'm collecting conkers

Leith Hill Music Festival, Dorking, Surrey

... The girls have just been singing at a music festival in Dorking. It is great fun. All the local schools put in a choir and they take it in turn to sing on the stage in front of a few hundred parents and then an adjudicator gives his comments on how they sang. There is a huge range of songs and also sizes of choirs. My children's school is large but welcomes all into the choir so the sound is always loud and cheerful with a variable level of tunefulness. Some of the local schools are tiny, one had about a dozen children on stage and that was the entire school. The most popular song of the morning was the conker song. Every last member of the choir had a huge grin on their face as they belted out the addictive words and music to:

Conkers! ... I'm collecting conkers,
I'm trying to find the biggest and the best

Conkers! ... Lots of lovely conkers,
I want a conker that's better than the rest

We all left the auditorium humming it and have been bursting in to song all day ...

Fun with conkers

Conkers are the seeds of the Horse Chestnut tree and come cased in a spiky shell. Though very familiar, they really are quite magical. Hunting through the long grass, when you come upon that spiky case and break it open, the rich mahogany of the nut bursts out. It is so ridiculously smooth and shiny with beautiful patterns embedded in it that it's hard to believe it's natural. The fact that the sheen is relatively short-lived only makes the moment of discovery all the more precious.

Just collecting conkers can be extremely satisfying and is usually a numbers game – the more the better. My children have enjoyed making families of the different sized conkers and tend to hoard them like squirrels. We regularly find suitcases full of mouldering husks of conkers through the winter months.

The classic conker game is hard to beat. Choosing your 'king' fighting conker, skewering it and hanging it on string is a ritualistic pastime carried out by children for millennia. When I was a child I remember pages of advice in magazines and books about how to make your conker a champion. I remember suggestions for drying them slowly in a warm oven or airing cupboard; soaking them in vinegar or brine. Author Roald Dahl swore by drying them slowly for more than a year until they were hard as bullets – he apparently achieved a 109-er with this technique! Nothing seemed to make much difference for me but it was great fun to fight and

see how long the conkers would last. Anything above a niner was a true veteran and Roald Dahl's record would be very hard to beat.

In case you can't remember these are the **basic rules of conkers**:

1 Player one holds up their conker, hanging on its string at arm's length.

2 Player two wraps their string around their hand pulls the conker back with the second hand and flicks it at player one's conker. You have to aim to hit the conker directly – no tangling round the string and ripping it off! If you do tangle strings then the players shout 'strings'. The first one to shout gets the next go.

3 You take it in turns to hit each other's conker. As soon as one conker breaks and falls off its string the game is over. The winning conker is then named, based on how many other conkers it has vanquished. On its first victory it is called a one-er; if it has beaten two conkers it is a two-er and so on.

So go out this autumn and have a game – try to keep it a good clean fight – I take no responsibility for any injuries. If you want to get really serious why not enter the World Conker Championships in Oundle, Cambridgeshire.

When I go to the woods my favourite game is 'To me'. You probably haven't heard of this game before, but then you shouldn't have because me and my family made it up! It's fun and a nice change to just walking forever and maybe a sit down on a damp, wet, cold log for two seconds and then some more walking.

'To me' is a game that you can play only if you have a big stick (light, not heavy), pinecones (or something similar), a big space with no trees in the way and most importantly a group of about four to eight energetic, ready for fun people who are willing to bring on the challenge.

The first challenger gets ready, stick in hand and concentrating-face on. And then it begins ... the other people (the throwers or the evil ones) start chucking the pinecones that they have collected from the forest floor at the challenger. As they viciously throw the pinecones they have to shout 'to me' really quickly (most important part of the game) then they throw the pinecone. The challenger has to turn to the thrower and bat all the flying pinecones coming towards them!

I've made 'to me' sound like a serious game but it's really not! And that's why 'To me' is my favourite game to play in the woods (you should try it too some day ;-P).

Zoe Almond age 11

Abinger Common, Friday Street, Surrey

... The woods around Friday Street havee a sizeable plantation of oaks, unusually with a field layer of bilberries. Like supermodels at a post-show party, the oaks are all uniformly slim with sinuous un-branching trunks wearing skin-tight mossy cocktail dresses. Further on the woods are more variable, of mixed age and species, with a wide diversity of shapes and sizes. At the moment we are collecting the alphabet and these woods are a rich source of material. Armed with a camera we have collected a high quality alphabet. We search out letters in patterns in the bark and the outline of trunks, branches and roots. We make our way through the alphabet on every walk; so as an on-going challenge we are trying to accumulate 'the ultimate alphabet', taking the best of the best from all our walks. Some of the letters are seriously good, I keep a folder with the best of each letter, replacing them as we find better examples.

While you are looking for the alphabet you may spot some other interesting shapes, symbols and pictures in the branches and bark markings to add in to your collection. Some woods are better than others for alphabet and symbol spotting. The older mixed deciduous woodland gives the best scope for gnarled trunks and roots and messages in the bark. Once you have photos of your woodland alphabet it can be fun to create messages and names to print out for birthdays ...

Games with sticks

Simonsbath, Exmoor

... Every walk deserves a stick. When I was younger we spent our Easter holidays on Exmoor and it was a great moment when my parents bought me my first thumb stick. We would go to visit a craftsman who collected fallen antlers from the moor. He would divide the antlers up sawing and smoothing the horn into satisfying thumb stick V's, as well as making whistles and key rings. The cut and smoothed antler was then attached to a long straight coppiced pole and a rubber ferrule pushed on the end. There was some talk of him using potato starch to attach the antler but I may be confused – it was about 30 years ago. My thumb stick had one prong that bent towards me over the inside of my thumb as I walked while the second was a similar circumference to the base of my thumb, perfect for my hand to wrap around and grasp. I loved that stick and for many years would not walk without it. Eventually I grew out of it and it dropped out of use. Recently I reclaimed it and my children took an interest in it. Unfortunately woodworm had taken over and it disintegrated into a pile of dust about half way down. I am now on the search for a nice straight coppiced pole of just the right dimensions to which the antler can be reattached ...

Games to play with sticks

Children are great stick collectors and any walk in the woods requires a multitude of special sticks. We have a collection of precious sticks parked outside our back door. These days the dog also collects sticks and to go with the children's special sticks we have a collection of half chewed sticks that he has brought home. It often causes problems when we meet children on walks and he whips their stick from their hands thinking they want to play; wails ensue as we try to extract the stick from the dog's mouth.

A stick has a life of its own in a child's hand. It may be just a thwacking stick, good for taking the heads off nettles and hacking

Spilikins Spilikins or pick up sticks requires a collection of at least 20 small twigs. They should be thin – about the thickness of an earthworm is good. We like to peel our sticks because it makes them a bit smoother which is better for the game, however, it can be quite fiddly so if you get fed up doing this then use them as they are.

Once you have the sticks, one player holds them in a bundle upright on the table in one hand and then lets go so the fall into a pile. Players then take it in turns to try to lift a stick off the pile without disturbing the other sticks. While the player is trying to lift a stick the other players are watching like hawks to see the slightest movement in the rest of the pile. If anything moves the stick has to be put back and the next player tries their luck at removing a stick. Play continues until all the sticks have been claimed. The player with the most sticks is the winner.

Sticky bread/marshmallows If you can have a fire at the end of the day, a walk in the woods is a great opportunity to collect some sticks for making sticky bread or toasting marshmallows.

As well as kindling to get the fire going and pinecones for popping and putting messages into (see Woodland messages on page 34), for cooking sticky bread and toasting marshmallows you want sticks at least a foot long, ideally a bit longer, about finger width at the holding end and tapering. Once collected and while you are waiting for the campfire to reach ideal cooking conditions – glowing embers, not too much flame – you should strip the bark off the twigs to ensure they are really clean for your food.

Marshmallows are always popular with children; the large bags of standard sized pink

their way through the jungle or it may be a wand to cast spells causing mayhem and madness all around. Numerous guns and *Dr Who*-inspired weaponry can be seen in passing sticks; a child's imagination in the woods has no boundaries. There are also many games and uses for sticks. If you need motivation while walking through the woods then some of these activities that require stick collection on the way can be a great excuse.

and white ones work best. Squidge a marshmallow onto the end of the stick and hold it over the glowing embers for half a minute or so. The marshmallow will heat up and melt on the inside while going crispy on the outside – that is my favourite. Leave it a bit longer and it will go brown. Some people like to eat the crispiness off and put it back in to crisp up the next layer and eat through the marshmallows in that way. Some people like to burn them to see them go black and shrivelled but they taste too charcoaly for me.

Even better than marshmallows is sticky bread. If you buy yourself a bag of bread mix you can be really lazy and it is very simple if you are camping. Mix up your bread dough and give each person a golf ball sized lump. Roll the dough into a snake and then twist it around your stick, squidging it on a bit if necessary to make sure it stays on. Then hold the twisted dough over the hottest bit of the fire and cook it until it sounds a bit hollow when you tap it. The best is to melt a bowl of butter (even better garlic butter) beside the fire while you are cooking so you can peel off strips of cooked sticky bread and dip it in the butter – delicious!

Stick jenga This is a game that Lottie and I devised one day when she was off school. We took Alfie for a walk in the woods and collected lots of short sticks. We started off with about 10 sticks each. We then sat on the ground and began to make a triangular tower, taking it in turns to add our sticks to the structure. When we had finished the first set of sticks we went to collect another 10 sticks each and then another 10 sticks. We kept on going until the tower became unstable and then collapsed.

How high can *you* go?

Story sticks This is a great activity for quite a wide age range. We used to do it as an activity in the infant school's very small woodland in Eco-club. Each person needs a stick with a few elastic bands twisted round it. While you are on your walk each person then collects anything they see that is of interest and attaches it to their stick by poking the item under the elastic band. Once the stick is full and the walk is over you can all sit down and look at your sticks and each person gets to talk about their stick and what they found and why they thought it was interesting, where it came from and anything else they want to say about their walk and the woodland they walked through.

Tracking

Hare and Hounds Tracking games are a great way to cover lots of ground with unwilling walkers. We will often suggest a walk with the kids and get moans of dissent; the same walk dressed up as a game of Hare and Hounds is met with cries of delight.

To play Hare and Hounds you need to split into two groups. The lead group are the Hares and will leave the trail while the following group are the Hounds who will try to follow the hares and hunt them down. You need at least one person in each group who is old enough and knows how to find the objective of the outing – if there is one. It is useful to have an idea of where you want to end up just in case your tracking skills are not great!

The hares get a head start; we usually reckon on about five minutes but it depends on terrain and the speed of the people in the two groups. Woodland is great for this game as the hares will be out of sight very quickly. You need to agree trail signs before you go but we usually keep it really simple and just use sticks and stones to make arrows.

Just keep going with as many side routes and detours as you think the players will enjoy and then all meet up at the end to have a picnic or some treats.

Nim's game For Nim's game you just need three small piles of twigs and two people. Set the twigs out in three rows, there can be any number of twigs in each row but we usually make it that the first row has three twigs, the second four twigs and the third five twigs. Now take it in turns to remove twigs. The rules are that you can only take from one row at a time, you have to take at least one twig but you can take more if you wish – as long as they are from the same row. The aim of the game is to make the other player take the last twig. It sounds simple but it is surprisingly challenging and often frustrating.

Look under logs

Holmesdale School Woods ... June

... Everyone is fully absorbed in the forthcoming Olympics: the torch is coming through town in a few days and we all have a bad case of Olympic fever. I was running Eco-club at the infant school today and decided to go with the theme and have an insect Olympics. First off we set out into the woods to find some woodlice. After some discussions we lifted some logs and in no time at all we had gathered ourselves a good supply.

I drew a circle on a piece of paper and turned the woodlouse pot upside down in the centre. One of the children was designated starter while another took charge of the pot. The starter made the commands: on your marks, get set, go; the pot holder lifted the pot and they were away. The children took their supporting roles seriously and screamed and shouted to the best of their ability. No one had any idea which woodlouse was which, but it didn't seem to matter. Names were made up and changed each race. Everyone had a go as starter and pot holder and the cheering never abated. Between races, the children, despite my protests, manhandled the woodlice and watched them curl into their defensive balls, some were released early and some attempts were made to smuggle favourite woodlice home but I think by the end the majority had made it back to their under-log homes, a little dazed and bewildered but I hope enlightened in the life of human sports stars. The kids were all wildly overexcited, thoroughly enthused and hoarse ...

How to find insects for races

Racing woodland animals can be a lot of fun and it can be enjoyable trying to find the competitors in the first place. Have a rummage around in the leaf litter, inspect some leaves, look under logs and prize up the bark on a dead tree, you will almost certainly find some bugs. Ones to look out for include: beetle larvae, spiders, millipedes, shield bugs, moths, wasps, worms, snails and slugs, ants, woodlice and a variety of beetles. There's no need to race the insects you find or even to touch them if you are a bit squeamish. If you do race them make sure you are nice to the competitors and put them back where you found them so they have some chance of survival.

The best racers I find are woodlice, beetles and snails. Maybe you could have an inter-species race and see which bug is fastest...

Racing woodland animals can be lots of fun, as can finding the competitors before you start. Make sure to handle them gently and put them back where you found them.

* Insects in woodland

The woods are a paradise for insects and other invertebrates that fulfil many important roles and niches in the woodland. They inhabit trees, living and dead, as well as other plants and leaf litter. They may be carnivores like the predatory beetles, spiders, lice, wasps, and millipedes; herbivores like the slugs and snails, spiders, beetles, butterflies, moths, bees and aphids; detritivores like some beetles, millipedes, hoppers and worms (earth, round and flat) or parasites on plant and animals like the round and flat worms, some bees, wasps and ants, flies, lice and mites. Many insects have larval stages that feed in a different part of the food web than their adult form.

In a simplified oak wood food web, Winter Moth caterpillars eat oak leaves on the trees while worms, slugs and snail and millipedes decompose the leaves on the ground. Predatory beetles attack and eat both the on-tree caterpillars and the decomposers on the ground. They, in turn are preyed on by mice, shrews and other small mammals. Owls, Foxes and Badgers hunt for the small mammals on their nightly rounds.

While insects form an integral part of the woodland ecosystem, recycling nutrients and assisting in plant reproduction they can also cause problems.

Some moths are known for their ability to eat the leaves off whole hillsides of trees. Thomas and Packham recount studies that investigated the devastation, by moths, of the oak canopy in woods near Kidderminster. In both 1979 and 1980 the oaks, Ash and Hazel were completely defoliated. Apparently the falling faeces of the caterpillars could be heard raining down through the trees and the trunks were dotted with silken parcels of caterpillars descending to pupate.

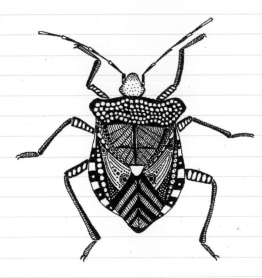

Insects can cause physical damage by eating shoots and by burrowing under bark but they also act as vectors of disease. Introduced species can be a particular problem if the usual controls, predatory and climatic, are absent. They can proliferate and can cause widespread and rapid damage. The European Elm Bark beetle was responsible for the spread of Dutch Elm Disease which destroyed more than 25 million trees from the late 1960s onward. The adult beetle carried the fungus from tree to tree while its larvae burrowed into the xylem taking the fungi with them, making the perfect entry point for the fungi to infect the tree. Without the help of the beetle the fungi would never have been able to penetrate the bark.

My cousins don't live far from us and we see them quite often. Spotlight is one of our favourite games, especially in the little wood in their back garden when it's growing dark and the adults are busy chatting inside.

What you need to play Spotlight is: a woodland area – or somewhere similar, a group of friends and a torch. We also include our cousins' tree platform in our game, but this is not crucial. This game is best played when it is dark and can be played with any number of people, but we enjoy it most with around four to eight players.

We select one person to be the spotlight and they take the torch up onto the tree platform (or just pick an area between you) and count to 30. Give the rest of the players a starting place a bit further into the woodland. They all hide while the spotlight is counting. Once they've counted to 30, they turn on the torch and scan the area for the hiding players. The aim for the hiding players is to reach the spotlight, without being seen. If the spotlight sees any players, they have to say their name and where they are hiding. If the spotlight gets the right name and hiding place, then you're out and you come and stand with them. But, if they say the wrong name or hiding place, you stay put. The game ends, either when a hiding player reaches the spotlight area or when the spotlight gets everyone out.

We spend ages out in the garden playing this game with our cousins. It's fun to see what works better, all working together to get to the spotlight or working individually. Just remember to wrap up warm.

Anousha Wardley, age 13

Talk to the birds

Juniper Hill Woods, North Downs ... February

... It's a crisp clear winter's day, one of the few we've had this year and I take my camera on my walk with Alfie. Along the edge of the wood, Redpolls are feasting on Old Man's Beard so I stalk and click, trying to capture the birds without scaring them away. Inevitably, I get too close and they rise in a Mexican wave and then, like arrows they arc across the fields to the safety of the far side of the hedge.

Up above I can hear the calls of a Blue Tit in the oak tree. It is hopping around with no regard for gravity, spinning its way in amongst the knobbly twigs in search of morsels so I focus on that for a while. As we continue our walk along the margins of the woods we can hear numerous small birds, twittering and trilling in conversation but they all move out of sight before we reach them. High above me I can hear the repetitive *pip-pip-pip* and faster pneumatic whistle of the Nuthatch. Peering up into the budding branches I can still hear it but see nothing. I keep watching and around the side of the trunk the aerodynamic head and body of the Nuthatch appears, its black beak extending into a go-faster stripe that reaches across the eye and down to the shoulder and the sunset pink of its underbelly blushing in the winter sunlight. Holding itself close to the trunk it walks up and down the tree in search of the insects that it wheedles out from under the bark. I track it for some time circling round trunks and darting to neighbouring trees but at every shutter release it ducks behind a leaf or twigs, utterly foiling my photographic attempts ...

How to talk to birds

Birds can be hard to see in woodland. You get the occasional flash of something as it flits between the branches but it is really hard to keep your eye on anything for long. The only way to keep a check on the birds that are present is by listening to their song. Luckily some of the key woodland birds have very characteristic calls and songs that make it a bit easier. Not only do they have distinctive calls, but it is actually possible to mimic them and sometimes they will reply.

Have a go at some of these calls and see if you can get talking to an owl or a woodpecker.

Hoot like an owl The classic hoot of an owl is the exclusive call of the Tawny Owl. Fortunately Tawny Owls tend to nest, roost and hunt in deciduous woodlands so this is a great place to try out your hooting and see if you can get an answer. Obviously owls are nocturnal so think about giving this a go at dusk or later to increase your chances.

Most birds can be hard to see in woodland; the only way to keep a check on them is by listening out for their very different songs and calls.

Hold your hands against each other palm-to-palm as if you are just about to say your prayers and then swivel your palms so that you can wrap your fingers round. Now push your palms apart, while keeping your fingers tightly wrapped to make an airtight chamber. Bend your thumb knuckles up, keeping the tips and heels tight together to create an eye-shaped opening into the airtight cavity between your hands. Make your mouth into a surprised 'O' shape and rest your relaxed top lip on the thumbs above the knuckle and the bottom lip lightly below the thumb knuckles. Blow into your hands and you should hear a wonderful rich owl's hoot. You may need to adjust your mouth and hands around a bit to get it to work but once you've got it you'll never forget it.

Go out at dusk near woodland and try out your hoot to see if you can get a reply.

This same technique can be used to make the calls of Woodpigeon and Collared Dove. Try to say the sentences below as you hoot and it should come out pretty well.

Woodpigeon – 'take two turns, Taffy.'

Collared Dove – 'united, united, united'

Knock on wood The Greater Spotted Woodpecker knocks on trees, particularly in spring, to advertise his territory. If you find yourself a good solid stick and bang it end on against a hollow tree trunk you may get an answer from a Greater Spotted Woodpecker. Spring is likely to be your best chance of success but they are here year round so you could be lucky at any time.

* Woodpeckers

The **GREEN WOODPECKER** is the largest of the three species of woodpecker in this country. It is distinctively green backed with a red Mohican down the centre of its forehead extending to the back of its neck. It has a hard, dagger-like bill for excavating its nest hole and can often be seen on open grass prodding around for ants. When it flies off you can see its bright yellow-green rump and trademark undulating flight. Its call is a distinctive laughing *yaffle* which you may recognise from Professor Yaffle from *Bagpuss*.

The **GREAT SPOTTED WOODPECKER** has a red cap and red under-tail, while its back, wings and head are marked in black and white. The Great Spotted Woodpecker drums on tree trunks to advertise its territory. It also uses its strong bill to pick insects larvae out of the wood and to excavate a hole. Like the Green it has an undulating flight.

The **LESSER SPOTTED WOODPECKER** is like a smaller, slightly faded out version of the Great Spotted Woodpecker and is easily overlooked.

When the woodpecker excavates its nest hole it hammers at a rate of 20 knocks a second with a force of 15mph. How does it manage this without injuring itself?

Woodpeckers are brilliantly adapted. Their breastbone has a very low keel so that they can hug the tree closely. Their legs are short and their claws widely spaced and backward facing and their tail feathers are very stiff, all of which provide a counterbalance to the knocking. Other adaptations help prevent damage to the brain and eyes. Firstly, they have perfect aim. They always hit the wood straight on so the force is always predictable. The bill is specially reinforced with a horn-like substance and hinged to the skull to absorb the impact. They have a spongy but very strong bone structure in their skull to absorb as much of the force as possible and having a rigid brain rather than one encased in liquid helps as the brain rattles around less. They also have extremely strong, responsive neck muscles that contract moments of a second before impact, acting as shock absorbers by directing some of the force down the back. They have a thick third eyelid that closes across the eye, holding the eyeball in its socket and preventing damage from shards of wood.

Thicket is a game that we learnt on our bonding days at school. It was made up by Mr Moses, our teacher, and we love it and still play it nearly every time we go to the woods. All you need are three or more enthusiastic hiders, and one ruthless hawk (not a real one!) Here's how to play:

Nominate one person to be the hawk, and a certain space that he/she is allowed in (normally about 2m by 2m), called the nest. The aim of the game is for the rest of the people to hide, within set boundaries, while the hawk counts with his or her eyes closed. Once the hawk has finished counting he has to spot the hiders without leaving the nest.

But don't worry, it's not that easy! It is a race between the hiders, to see who can get to the hawk's nest first. They will have to keep swapping hiding places, gradually getting closer to the hawks 'nest'. The game ends when, either someone gets to the nest, or everyone gets seen. The winner is the one who gets to the nest first, or the one who is last to be spotted.

You can make the game harder, by saying, for example, 'you have to peek your head out in the next five seconds' or 'you have to move hiding spots at least five times in this game'. You can similarly make it easier by saying things like 'the hawk is going to close his eyes for five seconds' or give the hiders 40 seconds to hide.

The best thing about Thicket is that is really quick, so it is easy to fit in if you don't have much time. Here are some tips to help you have the best game of Thicket you can possibly have:
• Make the 'nest' near a bench, rock, log or similar.
• Make sure you are playing in a place with lots of trees, bushes, rocks and hiding places.

Poppy Wardley, age 12

Obstacle courses

Wilderness Wood, Sussex ... July

... Sleeping in the horsebox last night I had the sensation I was at sea. The wind blowing in the canopy overhead ebbed and flowed, pulsing through the night. The rush of sound built as a wave of wind worked its way through the canopy towards us, reaching a crescendo, a tsunami of noise as it passed over battering the leaves and bending the coppiced branches. The horsebox dipped and swayed in response to the passing gusts adding further to the sensation. I felt like Pi in his lifeboat waiting for the roar of Richard Parker.

By the time we woke this morning the wind had died down and we were treated to a clear blue sky with whispers of wind playing in the leaves and rattling the springy coppices gently. We set out for adventure and found the perfect spot for making an obstacle course. Well-spaced trees with little undergrowth, a deep carpet of dry leaves and plenty of fallen branches and felled remains. We made the most awesome obstacle course and had loads of competitive races before moving on to some highly complex den building ...

How to make obstacle courses

Woodlands can be great places for obstacle courses. With all the materials at hand there are loads of options for setting up challenging and fun obstacles. These are some ideas:

● Use fallen trees as balance beams to walk along
● Felled cross sections of trunk make great stepping stones
● Felled or fallen thin branches stuck into the ground make slalom courses
● Mounds of leaves can be 'leaf pits' to jump over
● Balance long thin branches between trees or on stumps for hurdles or if they are too high, limbo
● A long strong branch balanced over a fallen log makes a good see-saw
● Branches laid on the ground make a ladder for quick foot running in each space,

· ·

These are just a few ideas but there are no end of other possibilities: I'm sure you can come up with loads more.

Take it in turns to race through the course, time yourself and see if you can get faster, race in teams or make two identical courses and race against each other. Most of all, have fun!

We set out on an adventure and soon found the perfect spot for making an obstacle course from the fallen branches and old logs. The leafy floor gave a soft landing.

When we go to the woods I love building Wigwams. You have to have at least three players. All the players have to stand in a line before the race. The timer starts the race by shouting, 'Go!' All the players race to their nearest tree with a low, strong branch and start gathering big branches and logs to build their wigwam. You need one long and strong branch to be the first piece — one end on the ground and one in the 'V' of where the branch joins the tree. You then get lots of branches and twigs and lay them against that first branch to build your wigwam.

You only have 30 minutes to build it, after which the timer shouts 'Finish!' All the players have to stop immediately whether they have finished or not. The timer judges all the wigwams by giving the players marks out of ten. To win, you have to have the neatest, densest Wigwam! The size doesn't matter though, so a good tip is to build it small so you are able to make it more dense but don't make it too small so that the timer cannot fit inside!

Imogen Almond aged 13

Look around you and then look again.
Let the woodland's gifts fire your imagnation.
Experiment with nature, try new skills and
develop your ideas to create something unique
from the woodland's great resources.

Be creative

Leaf prints

Holmesdale School Eco club

... Bang. Bang. Bang. The school hall echoes with the sounds of hammering and the head teacher has just come to see what is going on. We are making leaf prints with a difference. Rather than the traditional technique of painting your leaf and printing it onto paper, I have torn an old sheet into squares and brought in all the hammers I could find in our shed. This is the school's Eco-club that I help with on a Friday afternoon. Two children from each class get the chance to come and join us if they wish and each week we do some kind of 'eco' activity. This week, after putting the shredded paper into the compost bins and recording the number of bicycles and scooters in the racks, we head out into the woodland to collect some leaves. This activity requires freshly-picked, growing leaves so it is a rare occasion when we actually allow the kids to pick something. We steer them towards the interesting shapes and fleshiest leaves we can see but also collect a few of the waxy leaves and old dead leaves as well just to see what happens. Then back to the school hall as it is beginning to rain quite persistently. Each person gets their hammer and fabric and sandwiches the leaf between a fold of material before hammering away. The children delight in being allowed to make so much noise and have to be stopped from completely pulverising their leaves.

As we hammer we can see the juices of the leaves soaking through the material. When we stop hammering and peel off the squashed leaf the kids – and adults – are amazed to see beautiful leaf skeleton imprints on the fabric. It is immensely satisfying and extremely effective. Now we just need to think what to do with 40 or so leaf prints ...

How to make leaf prints

To make these permanent leaf prints you just need some cotton fabric – an old sheet torn into squares is perfect – a hammer and a suitable surface to hammer on. A wooden chopping board on the floor is works well if you need to protect your floor.

❶ Go out and find some leaves and try out lots of different shapes and textures to find out which give the best results. Cow parsleys and other similarly fleshy leaves work really well. Waxy leaves like Holly and other evergreens don't work so well but give them all a go, try some strongly-coloured autumn leaves and see how they work.

2 Hammer firmly all over the area of the leaf and make sure the head of the hammer is as flat as possible for the best effect.

3 Then open up the fold of fabric and peel away the squashed leaf and hey presto you have a leaf print. In fact you will have a double leaf print – one on the top layer of fabric as well as the bottom. This leaf print is more or less permanent – as you will know if you have ever tried to get grass stains out of your clothes – and can be used for a whole range of decorations.

••

Our ideas include cutting them out and sticking them on cards, putting a safety pin on the back for a brooch to sell at the school fair, putting them in frames as pictures. The person who showed me the technique had cut one out and stuck it on a hat as decoration and it looked fantastic. Some of the adults were so enamoured of the prints they are planning to decorate cushion covers and curtain edges.

If you don't have any suitable fabric, this technique can be carried out by sandwiching the leaves between sheets of paper almost as effectively.

* Leaf colour change and loss

In autumn, in response to the shortening day length, a hormone is released in deciduous trees which causes the cells between the leaf and the twig to break down and stop the flow of sap to the leaf – a process called abscission.

Without a supply of sap, photosynthesis ceases, along with the production of the green pigment, chlorophyll. Now the other true colour pigments which exist alongside the chlorophyll in the leaves – the yellow xanthophylls and orange beta carotenes – are able to have their moment in the limelight.

In the next stage, as the tree endeavours to withdraw to storage as much sugar from the leaves as possible, red anthocyanins are produced. These are a by-product of sugar and break down in the absence of phosphate which is usually maintained in the supply of sap. This chemical reaction requires bright light conditions which is why bright sunlight in autumn results in stronger red leaf colours. The red of the anthocyanins are not only seen in autumn leaves. The same chemical process occurs in new growth before the sap rises. This can be seen in the red colour at the edges of leaves and buds as they unfurl in bright spring sunlight as well as colouring on apples –

always the side exposed to the sun. The anthocyanins are water-soluble so, as the leaves dry out, the red colours fade leaving the brown of the oxidised tannins to dominate.

The final stage in leaf drop occurs when a cork layer forms between the leaf and twig and the leaf is released from the tree. Some trees, such as young beech trees, are unable to produce the cork layer so the dead leaves do not fall off; they dangle through the winter months until the new leaf growth displaces them.

Leaves will often show a range of colours throughout autumn. The oak leaf initially turns yellow, moves onto a reddish-brown, ending up dark brown as the combination of carotinoids, anthocyanins and oxidised tannins are exposed in sequence. The autumn colour a tree displays is affected by the chemical nature of the tree's leaves, soils under the tree and the levels of different nutrients (particularly magnesium, phosphorus, sodium and iron) the tree will absorb. The levels of tannin in the leaves, the acidity of the sap combined with the ambient weather conditions will all affect the colour displayed in the leaf – nature's litmus test.

Tyrrel's Wood, Norfolk, summer

... Tyrrel's Wood in Norfolk is an ancient woodland, possibly even a primary woodland that has been around since the retreat of the last Ice Age. Today I was struck by the patterns on the Hornbeam. Maybe they had been undergoing particularly rapid growth this year as they had particularly unusual and distinctive patterns, as if they were suffering from stretch marks. When you take the time to look closely at the bark of a tree and compare the different species, the most beautiful patterns, textures and timbres are displayed. The Ash was a subtle icy silver grey-green: cold and smooth it reminds me of the ice on a deep frozen river. The Yew's dark brown bark appears spongy on its fluted trunk from a distance but close up it has layer upon layer of flakes of leprous skin. The beech is a velvet smooth slate grey inviting the carvings you so often see; in older trees the bark seems to slump around side branches and old scars like a slow flowing river of mud, frozen in time. Birch bark is beautiful and ethereal in younger trees, the unicorn of the bark world; glowing white and silver with its contrasting black horseshoe marks around its stem, curling peels of the outer layers. In stark contrast to this the bark of the old oak tree is a completely different wonder, a living geology. The trunk of an oak tree displays chasms, crevasses and canyons to rival anything the Himalaya have to offer. Deep and dark, you could lose your fingers in the depths of the crenellations in the oak ...

How to make bark rubbings

Take a rubbing to capture the unique nature of a tree's bark. All you need is a wax crayon and some paper – not too thick or thin – a standard weight printer paper is ideal. Just lay your paper on the tree and rub over it with the flat side of your wax crayon. The crayon will pick up all the lumps and bumps, displaying the pattern of the bark on your paper.

You can use a similar technique to make a leaf rubbing. Put the leaf underneath the paper, vein side up and rub the flat side of the crayon over the top to reveal the midrib, veins and outline of the leaf. Use a different coloured crayon for the leaf on the same bit of paper you did its bark rubbing and you get a nice effect. The leaf and the bark pattern together should give you a good chance of identifying your tree. See the chapter on identifying your tree for some top tips.

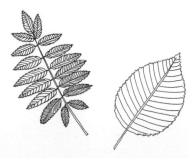

* Tree bark

Bark is a non-technical term for the outer skin of the tree that protects the phloem and xylem. The bark protects the tree from drying out, freezing and physical attack for example by fungi and other parasites.

On the outer surface of the phloem is a single layer of cells known as the cork, or bark cambium. These continually produce bark cells on their outer surface. Each tree's bark is unique. The chemical make up varies as does the thickness and the pattern of cracking and peeling which is dictated by the position of the cork cambium.

The thickness of the bark is very variable. The bark of the birch is very thin, just a papery skin while the bark of some pines, such as the redwood, can be as much as a foot thick. In trees such as the cork oak the cork layer is so thick it can be harvested without damaging the tree and used as a cork product.

Many trees have chemicals within their bark that enhance its protection. Birch bark is impregnated with volatile oils that deter insects and fungi; these oils also mean it makes a great fire lighter. It is so resistant to attack that tubes of bark are often found surviving long after the wood it was protecting has decayed. The bark of the oak is impregnated with tannins poisonous to insects that help protect the tree – these tannins were exploited for use in the leather tanning process.

Aspen bark is unique as it can photosynthesise; it has a green tinge and is attractive to grazing animals.

The bark of a tree changes considerably in some species as the tree ages. The bark of a young Ash tree is very smooth – significantly different from the mature tree which can be quite craggy. Similarly, the silvery white bark of the Silver Birch splits open and forms great black chasms such that the silvery layer is almost invisible in some older birch trees.

Bark and its extracts have been used for many different purposes including: cork, tanning and firelighting as well as cinnamon, quinine, and aspirin; the fibres have been used as cordage and birch bark is used as a waterproof sheet, most notably for canoe coverings.

Woodland art

Surrey Sculpture Park, Churt

... Surrey Sculpture Park is a great eclectic collection of sculptures, set in 10 acres of wooded valley. When you arrive you are given laminated sheets that take you on four coloured trails through the park. Sculptures line the paths and each sculpture is numbered and named along with the name of the sculptor and its price. Before long the girls devised a game where they took it in turns to guess the names of the sculptures. Then we took it in turns to choose the name of a sculpture in the next 10 and the others had to identify which sculpture it was. First up was a sculpture called 'splat'. We walked along investigating each sculpture and assessing it to see if it could feasibly be a 'splat', until we emerged into a clearing and there she was – a 15m long wooden girl lying flat on her face with her arms out above her head as if she had just tripped over a tree stump – 'splat' ...

How to make woodland art

Woodlands provide some inspiring materials if you are feeling creative. Autumn leaves have wonderful graduating colours; spring flowers may provide a block of colour; twigs and pine cones, sycamore seeds, beech masts and all the other bits and pieces of woodland flotsam and jetsam can all go towards making great sculptures.

I like to try ways of weaving leaves and twigs

together. I particularly enjoy peeling the bark off twigs so that they are clean and smooth to contrast with the craggy bark and give a wonderful finish to a sculpture.

Using nothing but the materials you find around you, you can make pictures or abstract designs and aesthetically pleasing patterns. It is immensely rewarding to take some time and make something eye catching in just a few minutes. Stop a while and think about what you can see and what you could make with it – you will open your eyes to all the colours and textures and materials that nature has to offer. In the process you will learn something about the materials, their opportunities and their limitations – and maybe some of your own.

Without glue or string you can use evergreen sap and thorns of the Blackthorn or Hawthorn or small sections of twig to join materials together. To join leaves you can thread the stalk of one leaf through the flesh of another.

Take some time to make
something eye-catching to
entrance the next passer by.
Anything can be a canvas: the
woodland floor or a crevice
in a tree trunk.

If you are feeling a bit more adventurous you can often find felled trees and branches with intact bark to try some bark art. Some barks can be peeled off in great strips or even whole tubes, Ash bark can be particularly good for strips while Hazel bark can be slid off sections of branches if you tap a section all around to loosen it first. To

Sculpture parks

There are many wonderful sculpture parks, some in public woodlands and some in private gardens. The botanical gardens also have temporary exhibitions as well as do National Trust properties. Keep your eyes open as you drive around the country as well as searching out advertisements in local papers and magazines. For ideas on where to see sculpture, look on www.bbk.ac.uk/sculptureparks/ which is Birkbeck University's International Directory of Sculpture Parks and Gardens. Using the techniques employed by tree surgeons, our instructor Roland, from the recreational climbing company Treefrog, spent a couple of days teaching us all the rope skills we would need to be able to climb safely into the tree canopy.

Other parks to search out include: **Grizedale Forest Park**, Coniston, Cumbria • **Hannah Pescher**, Ockley, Surrey • **Yorkshire Sculpture Park**, Wakefield, West Yorkshire • **Royal Botanical Gardens**, Kew, London • **Pride of the Valley Sculpture Park**, Churt, Surrey • **Forest of Dean Sculpture Park**, Gloucestershire • **The Wildart Trail**, Canterbury, Kent • **Hainault Forest Monster Trail**, Chigwell, Essex • **Kielder Water Forest Trail**, Northumberland

help with stripping the bark, find or make a choc or spud out of a wedge of wood to help ease the bark away from the trunk as you peel. Otherwise it is quite tough on your hands.

These natural works of art are temporary and ephemeral. Even if you can take them with you they will often decay and collapse so make sure you take a camera with you to capture your creations before you go. When you photograph them make the most of the setting; clear away extraneous debris from around your sculpture so it stands out. Use the weather and light to make the most of the picture, maybe there are shadows to enhance the shape or take the picture at night against a dark sky.

Time can really fly when you are making things in the wood so make sure you take food supplies to keep you going.

Park Hill Woods, Reigate ... December

... Honestly, kids – sometimes it takes a mini tantrum just to get out of the house – and that's just from me! However, once outside we are all smiles again and heading to the woods to make our annual attempt at wreath construction. I have an aversion to readymade wreaths, so each year, at great risk to our soft winter hands we wrestle Holly, ivy, spruce and any other winter greenery we can find into a circular shape. This year I have a cunning plan; based on a technique employed in building circular brush wood shelters. I can't remember where I saw it but I think it should work on a smaller scale for the wreath.

We start off by collecting thumb thick sticks as we walk up into the woods. We are looking for good holly bushes and ivy growths as we go and even some mistletoe. We seem to have picked a bit of the wood with very little ivy but there are some great holly bushes so we settle for that. Poppy and Lottie are in great form now and fully engaged in the prospect of wreath making. We collect our materials and then settle down to making the wreath. We have amassed a mountain of material and Lottie has a plan for a minimalist wreath so we decide to make two wreaths to decorate both the front and back doors. We stay out much longer than we originally thought, even missing our lunch, but return home with two gorgeous wreaths as our booty. Anousha spritzes the Holly one with silver spray just to finish it off and we are all happy with our handiwork ...

How to make your wreaths

❶ Collect 12–20 thumb-thick twigs to make the frame. Clear away leaf litter from a patch of soil and push the sticks into the ground in two concentric rings – the shape between the rings will be your wreath so size accordingly. We tend to go for the inner one about the size of a dinner plate, the outer one a few inches bigger.

❷ Collect your flexible greenery for the wreath base – ivy and Holly are ideal or you could go rustic and have bare twigs.

❸ Bend the twigs into circles between the two rings of sticks in the ground. You can tuck the ends in or twist them round each other to keep it all together a bit.

❹ Once your ring is as lush as you would like it twist stems of woody climbers – ivy, clematis, honeysuckle – or string round the doughnut shape to bind it all together.

❺ You can then lift your wreath out of its constraining circles and it should hold together. You can now decorate it by sticking in more vegetation, pine cones or tying on ribbons as you see fit.

❻ Finally, tie on a loop of string or ribbon for ease of hanging and Hey presto you have a wreath!

✳ The holly, the ivy and the mistletoe

HOLLY (ILEX AQUIFOLIUM) The European Holly is the winter king of the woods. In Celtic times the Holly King would rule from the summer solstice to the winter solstice at which point the Oak King would take charge.

The Holly tree or bush has distinctive evergreen leaves bearing spikes on its lower branches – above grazing height the leaves are without spikes. Being one of the few winter green plants the Holly was used extensively for grazing of animals. Winter fodder was largely provided by the pollarding and cutting of the less spiky higher branches. The berries, which grow only on the female trees, provide winter food for birds although birds that gorge on the berries have been known to die from inebriation as the berries ferment in their crop.

The festive link with Holly goes back to pagan times. Holly was often bought inside to ward off evil and protect against witchcraft; it was also a fertility symbol. The thorny crown and the blood red berries tie in nicely with the Christian story of Christmas and so the pagan habits of bringing holly in for Christmas decoration was easily incorporated into Christian traditions when they took over from pagan beliefs.

The Holly has long had associations with lightening and storms and is linked with Thor in Norse mythology; it was often planted near houses to protect against lightening strikes. In recent years scientists have shown that the prickles can in fact act as lightening conductors, suggesting they may actually afford protection to larger trees and buildings in their vicinity.

IVY (HEDERA HELIX) Hedera helix the Common or English Ivy is a woody climbing plant that uses small millipede-like aerial roots to fix the shoot to whatever it is climbing up. Ivies will climb up any solid structure and in woodlands can be seen climbing up trees to a height of 30m or more.

Their nectar and seeds are very important sources of food in the woodland and they are often alive with the rustling of birds and insects.

Although it often looks as though ivy is smothering trees it usually causes them no harm, as it is just using the trees as a structure to climb up. The greatest danger to the tree is competition over water and nutrient supply at the roots, however, its great weight can lead to wind-blow damage and dead trees can often fall under the weight of the ivy growing over it.

Ivy is used in Christmas decorations simply as a winter green for decoration. In Greek mythology ivy was thought to counteract intoxication, which is why Dionysus (the God of wine and revelry) is often depicted with ivy bound into his headdress with vines.

MISTLETOE (VISCUM ALBUM) Looking like a loosely-woven bird's nest suspended in the outer branches of the tree the mistletoe is parasitic on its tree host. It has specialised roots that penetrate the tree bark and extract nutrients from the tree. Mistletoe can grow on a wide range of trees and has been blamed for slowing a tree's growth, although only extreme infestations will have a significant impact on the host tree.

Mistletoe seeds are eaten by birds – typically the Mistle Thrush – and either the sticky seed is squeezed out and wiped off the bill directly onto the twig or is dropped in the faeces, the seed then sprouts and forms the mistletoe ball.

Mistletoe has recently been identified as a keystone species that has a big impact on the health and diversity of woodland communities. Areas with high mistletoe density support much greater diversities of animals than those without.

In the past mistletoe was seen as a symbol of divine fertility; the Celts saw it as a cure for barrenness. This may have led to the current tradition of kissing under the mistletoe at Christmas. Mistletoe was seen as particularly sacred by the ancient druids – particularly if grown on apple or oak.

Make nests

Holmesdale School Woods, Surrey

... Walking up the hill today I came across the remains of someone's hedge trimming. Lying in amongst the debris of branches sat a moss-lined nest. It was absolutely perfect, although obviously old and currently unused. This inspired me for an activity at Eco club this week. I took the nest in to show the children who were all entranced by its perfectly round shape, intricately woven twigs and warm, snuggly moss-lined cup. After collecting their class mascots we all headed out to the camp in the woodland and in small groups went to find materials that would be good for nest making. We found long, thin, whippy hazel twigs, trailing strands of ivy and bindweed as well as some clematis. There were cushions of spongy green moss and some old leaves and downy feathers we thought might make the ideal soft, warm nest linings.

Making the nests was quite a challenge. I don't know how birds manage with just a couple of beaks but even with six hands our finished products were nowhere near as proficient as the real thing – rather more plate-like than a nice enclosing cosy cup. Nevertheless, we were very proud and the mascots looked quite cosy nestled into (or onto) them. The children took them back to their classes to show off to their friends and teachers and then they went on display with the real nest as comparison ...

How to make a nest

Birds make nests for shelter and warmth so they can lay their eggs and raise their chicks in safety. They put them well out of reach in amongst a dense hedge or high in a tree to keep them as safe from predators as possible. Most woodland birds start the process by weaving a rough nest shape usually with twigs and grasses and then they sit in it pushing their bodies down to create the right shape. They continue to weave in grasses and twigs, often incorporating lichen and sheep's wool and mosses to insulate it to keep themselves and their offspring really warm. You may find man-made materials woven into nests as well, bits of string and fabric and even plastics find their way there.

When you are in the woods look for materials to make a good nest. You could take a toy or make a model to build the nest around. You could even make a nest for a person if someone fancies being a surrogate bird. Alternatively, just use your hand as a size guide and to push out the right shape. Think about how the bird would go about making its nest and how laborious and painstaking the process is for them – hundreds of journeys to find the materials, and just a beak to work with.

Like the birds, start with the base of the nest and weave the rough shape out of bendy twigs,

stems and grasses. Some of the woody climbers like clematis but also ivy and bindweed can be great base materials. Once you have your basic shape, keep adding in grasses and small twigs until you have quite a dense weave. Then you can start adding the insulation. Cushions of moss around the base of trees as well as lichen, and even fluffy seed heads at the right time of year will all make the nest cosy. If you are lucky you may find animal hair,

sheep's wool or some downy feathers to make a really snug nest.

Once you have made the nest see if you can find a good place to put it out of sight and reach of predators.

As well as nests made of twigs and moss you could try making mud nests if there is a handy puddle nearby – it's perfect if you are on clay soil. If your mud doesn't stick too well you could try mixing in some grass to bind it together better. You can hang them from under the crook of a large branch on a good-sized tree. Think about how a House Martin makes its nest. Take pea-sized balls of mud and build up the shape slowly, remembering to leave a door for getting in and out.

Build dens

Beechy Wood, Norbury Park, Surrey

... Last night I was cooking supper when Lottie walked in looking a bit green, her hands went up to her mouth and a panicked, rabbit in the headlights expression appeared in her eyes. I looked around desperately for an empty receptacle – a pint glass – which I shoved under her chin, she was immediately sick, filling it to the rim. At this precise moment Duncan arrived home with a friend, hot off the train from London in their dark suits. This friend had never been to our house before (or since strangely) so I was just welcoming him, still holding a pint glass full of vomit when Poppy wandered in, 'Mum, Alfie [the dog] has just been sick on my guitar case.' Much hysterical laughter and babble ensued as I tried to clean up the vomit from all areas and make offers of drinks and comfortable chairs.

Anyway the upshot of this is that I have one bright eyed and bushy tailed child at home today, unwelcome at school for 48 hours. Since she is on enforced leave and I need to take Alfie out we head out to Norbury Park which has some lovely areas of woodland. While there we have a wonderful time inventing games, climbing trees and building fairy dens. All very educational ...

How to build dens

Den building must be one of the most popular woodland activities for adults and kids alike. It is an instinctive desire to build a shelter in the wild to create a safe and secure environment for yourself, your friends and family. Everyone can join in and contribute to making the perfect den. There are many den building techniques I have seen employed and everyone has a favourite. Some techniques work better in some woods than others, depending on the materials that are available. Some woodlands have cut branches hanging around which greatly aid the process, while in others you will have to scrabble around for materials a bit more. Woodlands are much better these days since management techniques tend to leave branches and trees where they fall rather than tidying them away as they used to. The reason they are left is because of their great value as perfect woodland habitat for all kinds of little bugs and critters; however they are also very useful for den building.

Don't abuse the woods

If you were building a serious and semi-permanent shelter you would cut the appropriate materials from the woodland, but since you are just doing this for fun this activity should only use fallen or felled logs and branches that are all around you. You should never allow anyone to start pulling branches from living trees.

It is a natural desire to build
a shelter in the wild to create
a safe haven for yourself and
your family. Make your own
full-size retreat or a small
one for a fairy.

DIFFERENT KINDS OF DENS

The basic structure of a den usually makes use of a standing tree or horizontal branch on which to build a wigwam style hut around.

To make a wigwam chose a tree to be central pole and lean long, solid fallen branches all around. The length of the branches will dictate the size your shelter can be.

Most other den styles have a ridge pole. This can either lean on a branch or crook in a tree at one end and then slope down to the ground for a sloping ridge tent. Against this central ridge you then lean smaller branches along its length to create the sides of the den. This den shape will be high at its opening and then get smaller and smaller until it reaches the ground. The benefit of this design is that it requires only one branch to lean the ridge on and only relatively few long poles at the opening of the den.

The next most complex structure would be a long ridge pole balanced between two trees. This relies on two appropriately spaced trees with conveniently placed crooks. If you happen to have this situation you can make a very spacious den but you will also require a good supply of decent length branches to make the sides.

If you are feeling brave a more complex structure is a free-standing ridge tent design, something like Eeyore's house in *Winnie the Pooh*. This more sophisticated design requires two tripod structures to support each end of the ridge pole. It can be a challenging structure to balance the pole in a stable fashion without the use of string or rope.

Once you have the basic structure of the shelter you can fill in gaps with leaves and moss

or even mud mixed with grass to make a really weather proof structure if you feel so inclined. Embellishments such as seats, fireplaces and gardens can be added ad infinitum.

There is nothing more satisfying than building your own home and the feeling of self-sufficiency is great – even if the den is rickety and cold and draughty. We love going back to old dens, improving on them or changing them slightly each time we visit.

FAIRY DENS

If you are not in the mood for a full-scale construction then it can be fun to make fairy dens. Small children in particular may enjoy this activity as they can make their very own mini den without adult involvement. These mini structures are a great way to learn your den building skills without having to drag heavy branches around. These skills can then be scaled up at a later date.

Whittling

Caswell Wood, Wye Valley

... Poppy and Thea have sharp new penknives for their birthday and we are camping this weekend on the edge of the Forest of Dean, so we have the perfect opportunity for a bit of woodcraft and whittling. Diggory also has his penknife and is a prolific and experienced whittler so they are all settled round last night's campfire remains with sticks they collected earlier today. In their semicircle, leaning forwards, elbows on knees they are each creating little piles of wood curls around their feet. The smell coming off the newly-cut wood is powerfully resinous and the looks of concentration on their faces shows how absorbed they are by their tasks. I haven't been asked for food once in the last half hour, which must be a record, and aside from the occasional muttered comment there is almost complete, absorbed silence ...

How to whittle

Just smoothing the bark off wood and chipping away at it can be very satisfying and is good practice in terms of knifemanship. Once you have become a bit proficient you can try whittling and carving all sorts of things. Some little exercises like making a point on a stick or fashioning a flat spatula shape are all good skills to practise and will help when you come to want to make something more practical. Try to make a butter knife or make some little models.

These are a couple of simple whittling challenges which are easily achievable and either fun or useful as well.

MAKE SOME TONGS

Tongs are relatively simple to make and are extremely useful if you are going to be doing some campfire cooking.

● Find a 50cm long straight stick around 2cm in diameter. Ideally it should have some kind of a fork or knot at one end.

● Stand the stick fork end down and make a split in the top of the stick, as centrally as possible with your knife.

● Work the split down through the stick by wiggling and twisting your knife and by tapping it with another heavier stick. Once you can get your fingers into the split you can discard the knife and pull the two sides apart with your hands. If the split tries to run off to one side try to bend the thicker prong further back as you increase the split.

● Once the split is long enough or stops at the fork, wedge a small twig into the end of the split

Knife safety

● IN GENERAL, SHARP KNIVES SHOULD ONLY BE USED BY CHILDREN WHO ARE SEVEN YEARS OF AGE OR OLDER, AND ALWAYS UNDER CLOSE SUPERVISION.

● ALWAYS USE A SHARP KNIFE: THE MORE YOU HAVE TO FORCE A BLUNT KNIFE THE LESS CONTROL YOU HAVE OVER IT.

● ALWAYS CUT AWAY FROM YOUR BODY.

● WORK IN SHORT BURSTS: 30 MINUTES TO AN HOUR IS TOPS.

● MOVE THE WOOD, NOT THE KNIFE, TO MAINTAIN CONTROL.

and you have your tongs. You can make them last longer by lashing around the two prongs, just above the twig wedge. If you are really smart and you are using willow or another wood that the bark comes off easily you can use strips of the bark to lash around the tongs.

MAKE AN ELDER OR WILLOW WHISTLE – OR PEASHOOTER

● You will need a length of growing Elder or willow about a finger's width in diameter and at least 10cm long. Cut a notch in the bark at the top about an inch down from what will be the mouthpiece end.

● If you are using willow, tap all over the bark to loosen it and you should then be able to slide the pith out. If you have elder the pith is soft and can be scooped and pushed out using a smaller twig or long thin implement.

● Take the pith that came from the notch to the mouthpiece and flatten off one side and then reinsert the pith into the mouthpiece end of your bark tube. Align the flattened side with the notch. If you are using elder the pith will have

disintegrated so you need to find a length of twig of just the right diameter to use.

● You should now be able to blow down your whistle and get a sound. In the same way that you have to adjust your mouth when you whistle you may have to do a bit of jiggery pokery with the returned pith and your notch hole to get the whistle working really well. Your whistle is now ready to use.

● If you reinsert the rest of the pith in the open bottom end of the whistle and slide it back and forth you can play tunes on your whistle, rather like a trombone.

● To make a pea shooter, don't make a notch, just hollow out the Elder or willow bark tube, and hey presto it's done.

* Specialist woodcrafts

Different woods have been used for different purposes throughout human history. Most jobs can be done with any wood and historically people made do with the trees that were growing in their local woods. Over the years, however, it became apparent that certain woods suited particular tasks better than others. This led to some areas specialising in trades that suited their local trees and even later, plantations were set up to enable a craft or trade to develop. Roger Deakin (2008) talks of several specialist wood trades.

WALNUT VENEER Walnut has long been prized in cabinet making for the beauty of its wood, in particular the distinctive pattern and colour of the wood of the burr. A burr only develops in one tree out of a thousand and is an area of conflict in the wood growth, a kind of benign tumour, usually occurring where the root meets the trunk. When harvesting, the tree, usually more than 80 years old is uprooted, rather than felled, as the burr grows so low down. The burr is then extracted from the tree and thin sliced like Parma ham to half a millimetre thick and used as a veneer in high-value furniture and car dashboards. Jaguar cars are particularly known for the walnut wood veneer finish of their interiors. Walnut burrs are so valuable that individual burrs can change hands for up to £10,000 uncut. Once cut they can be worth £100,000 or even more.

CRICKET-BAT WILLOW The knock of leather on willow is one of the quintessential sounds of the English summer. The village green with white clad cricketers is still something you can see on weekend afternoons throughout the country. The wood used for cricket bats always comes from the willow, and not just any willow. Cricket bats throughout the world are nearly all made from the Cricket-bat Willows (*Salix alba* 'Caerulea') growing in Suffolk and Essex. It is apparently a source of great frustration to our fierce cricketing competitors, the Australians, that the willows grown down under do not yield the right density of wood to produce a top quality cricket bat. Without the perfect growing conditions the trees grow at the wrong speed and need constant watering to approximate the riverside conditions in which they grow naturally in eastern England and the resulting bats just do not fit the bill.

CHARCOAL Producing charcoal is an ancient woodland art that used to be seen in every wood. All hardwoods were therefore used for charcoal. These days charcoal is made primarily for the home barbecue trade although charcoal is still used by some blacksmiths as it burns at a higher temperature than the coke they would otherwise use. The best woods are hard woods which have a slow burn. To make charcoal you need a carefully controlled incomplete burn so that the integrity of the wood is maintained, the wood dries out but still has plenty of burn in it. All hardwoods can be used for charcoal but oak and hornbeam are ideal. Artists charcoal is a high value market and requires a particular consistency for which willow is usually used (spindle and oak are occasionally used (Ben Law 2008)).

BOX WOOD The wood of the Box tree is highly favoured by artists making fine wood engravings because cuts can be made in any direction and the wood holds the carving tool perfectly. Cross-cut box wood is particularly hard, dense and grainless because it grows so slowly that the rings are barely visible. Woodcuts (as opposed to wood engravings) use the side grain of the wood rather than the endgrain and can not produce artwork with such fine detail. Box wood is almost impossible to get hold of in the UK now, so many artists are using alternatives such as PVC or resin mounted on MDF.

Other woods also have or had specialist uses. The tall straight growth of pine trees was ideal for ships masts while the strong flexible wood of the Yew was known to be the best for the longbow.

Four Sticks Wood, Hainford, Norfolk

... At my grandparents' old smallholding in Norfolk, there are always plenty of children visiting and every time I go into the shed there seems to be a new crop of bows behind the door. Today is no different. As I creak open the door I am first struck by a billow of warm air, infused with the scent of oily rag and the metallic base-notes of agricultural machinery, I am then confronted by a new stand of bows, lovingly created and propped against the corrugated iron wall. Beyond the bows, in the gloom, the wall is slung with a swinging curtain of tools in varying states of sharpness and decay. Some of the tools date back to the days when my grandfather was farming. There are scythes, loppers, billhooks, parrot beaks, shears and edgers. There is something about the craftsmanship involved in these tools that attracts me – or maybe it is just the nostalgia for the time I spent at my grandparents in my childhood and I love to have a go at scything nettles whenever I am there. It is very hard work, partly because my technique is so poor and I have to banish children and animals from my vicinity for their safety, but it is extremely satisfying seeing the nettles laid down flat after taking a swing, it also makes me feel very rustic and wholesome ...

How to make your own bow and arrow

A basic bow is very easy to make with a penknife and a length of string.

FIRST THE BOW

❶ Cut yourself a length of hazel or other young flexible wood. It should be about shoulder height, and fairly consistently 2–2.5cm thick along its length.

❷ Cut a notch about 2cm in from each end. Tie the string onto one end using the notch to hold the string and prevent it from slipping. Turn the bow over and bend the wood so you have a nice bow shape and the tie the string tightly onto the notch at the other end. It can be

easier if you have two people at this stage, then one person can bend the bow while the other ties the string.

❸ You have a bow!

NOW MAKE THE ARROWS

❶ Use shorter, thinner lengths of hazel – roughly a forearm length long and finger diameter.

Strip the bark from the arrows – it makes it easier to find them again.

❷ If you want to be really smart you can find feathers and tie or tape them on to the end of your arrow.

❸ Put a groove into the end of your arrow for the bowstring. If you are using a feather this should run in the same direction as the groove.

Make a good supply of arrows, as they can be hard to find once fired. To make it easier you can tie a small length of brightly coloured ribbon to the back end so they show up in the undergrowth – they look great as they fly too!

Safety tips

THESE ARROWS CAN GO A SURPRISINGLY LONG DISTANCE AND WITH SOME FORCE SO NEVER SHOOT TOWARDS PEOPLE OR ANIMALS. GET SOME TARGET PRACTICE WITH TREES OR DRAW A TARGET AND MOUNT IT ON TREES OR STRAW BALES. YOU COULD EVEN TIE A STRING ONTO THE END OF YOUR ARROW AND SEE IF YOU CAN SHOOT IT OVER A BRANCH TO MAKE A ROPE SWING.

Take a camera

Nut Wood, Gatton Park, Surrey

... Thea had a friend round today, a lovely girl, very confident and outgoing; probably destined for the stage but I imagine she doesn't spend too much of her life in the outdoors. It was a beautiful day, so I suggested we took the camera and went to the woods. We had two hours before we had to pick up Lottie so we got stuck in. The girls competed for time in front of and behind the camera. We tried to get pictures of them jumping off logs as well as balancing and walking past each other. We tried some comedy shots and some atmospheric shots. We were so engrossed we didn't realise how late it was and had to run for it to get to Lottie in time ...

Things to try with a camera

Having a camera with you in the woods can completely transform your day. Everyone loves a photo and it can be a particularly good focus for older children (and some adults). For tweenagers and teenagers technology is all, so rather than rail against it, go with the flow and make it a positive addition to the woodland.

In these days of digital cameras there is no limit to the number of pictures you can take. Many cameras have a multitude of settings to try

out and you can trick even simple phone and digital cameras by shielding their light sensors to create different effects.

I remember trying to photograph a sunset from an aeroplane many years ago. I had a digital camera with lots of shutter speed and aperture settings but I had no idea what they all meant. By a process of trial and error – taking a photo, making adjustments and taking another – and gradually refining the settings, I was able to achieve the perfect shot.

Try some special effects as you take pictures, zoom in on someone's face and leave the background blurred or focus on a branch and leave the person out of focus. Try to move the camera alongside a fast moving person – for example on a swing to give the impression of speed as the background blurs or keep the camera still and the background sharp with the swinger whooshing through in a blur of colour.

Try putting colour films in front of the camera lens. Coloured wrappings from around flowers or sweets work well. Alternatively, put them over the flash so that you get a wash of coloured light. For this mushroom picture I put my hand over the

For tweenagers and teenagers technology is all, so rather than rail against it, go with the flow and make your use of it a positive addition to your woodland experience.

flash so it gave a reddish glow to the picture instead of a fully lit image. If you have a basic phone or digital camera it should have a light sensor. Try covering it up with your hand or a bit of tape. This will trick the camera into thinking it is darker than it is and the shutter will stay open for longer.

Kids love to take comedy shots and camera trickery. Stretch bodies up a tree; make a pile of heads. There are lots of ways to keep yourself entertained with a group of people a camera and some trees.

After the event you can have almost as much fun with your pictures. Just looking at the photos will bring back memories of the day but there is so much more you can do with digital images. Fiddling around creatively on the computer after a day out can produce some great results. There is a plethora of free software and apps to allow you to manipulate your pictures; cutting, editing, colour changes, making videos, digital collages. On the long cold winter evenings you can remember the fun you had outdoors when it is no longer possible to be there.

Be curious

Be really inquisitive; think about what you are seeing and hearing. Try investigating a little further to find out exactly what is going on under your feet, on the tree trunks and high up in the canopy. Which animals and plants can be found in your wood – and why?

Four Sticks Wood, Hainford, Norfolk

… Wellies on, swishing through the long grass, small clouds of micro moths dance around our knees as we walk. The tough stems of the much-maligned ragwort bind themselves into the grasses and form a perfect trip wire that holds your legs back as you try to move forwards. It is the stuff of the kind of dreams where everything hampers basic movement.

It also reminds me of the tales my father used to tell of his memories of the Blitz in Norwich when his school was evacuated to the girls' school. Apparently they would sit on the grass and tie knots in the grass stems so that when the girls came out to play they would trip over them.

Looking down onto the ragwort heads, many of them seem to be alive and wriggling with the black and yellow stripes of the Cinnabar Moth caterpillars.

Some of the newly-planted small trees are being choked by the grasses so we pull out the tough stems from around the young trees to give them some breathing space. By giving them a little less competition for water and nutrients, we are hopefully increasing their chances of survival in this very sandy soil. As we go, Mum helps me identify the different tree species. Most trees have some distinguishing feature, particularly distinctive leaves, bark, fruit, seeds or even buds but if it is the wrong time of year for that feature, or they are young trees, they can be hard to identify …

Tips on identifying trees

Identifying trees in all seasons takes a bit of practice, but if the mere mention of the subject makes you break into a cold sweat – don't panic – there is no need. Tree identification relies on skills that we learned as toddlers. Think about the games where babies are encouraged to match colours and shapes: tree identification is just an extension of those skills.

To start the process, have a look at the whole tree. Expert birders look for something in birds that they call their 'jizz'; something unique about

the bird that helps them identify it. It may be a particularly distinctive feature – like the blue flash on the side of the Jay, or it may just be something about the way the bird behaves, a general impression, such as the way a Sparrowhawk quarters a field while hunting. Look for the 'jizz' in the tree you are trying to identify. What stands out about it; what is your gut instinct?

Key features of your tree

Then take a closer look at specific features. The bark: is it smooth, rough, cracked into diamonds, spiralling, silvery, peeling? Similarly the leaf shape: are they simple, compound, palmate, needles, lobed, toothed or smooth edged? Are there any seeds, flowers or fruits to help differentiate your tree. All the time you should be flicking through your mental memory bank of shapes and patterns trying to eliminate certain possibilities and tie it all together. If the branches are bare look under the tree to see the fallen leaves along with any fruit, nut and seed remains. Sometimes there can be a confusing mix so check out the surrounding trees to work out which one the different leaves are likely to be from to narrow down your particular tree.

Often you can follow a kind of flow chart in your mind – 'smooth bark, OK it's not oak or either of the chestnuts, none of the conifers or willows ...; have a look at the leaves, small oval compound – could be Rowan or Ash; have a look on the ground, there are seed keys scattered around – definitely Ash ... job done!'

On the following page are the killer identifiers that I rely on to help me with identification. It is not comprehensive table but will help with identifying your tree from its 'jizz'. The Field Studies Council publishes an excellent foldout, laminated chart called 'The Tree Name Trail' that can be found on their website – www.field-studies-council.org A good website for ID is the Woodland Trust site – www.british-trees.com/treeguide and there are mobile phone apps and books that can help when you are in the field.

The table overleaf includes mostly native trees found in woodlands and I have assumed that you can distinguish between evergreen and deciduous trees. I have included Sycamore, a non-native, as it is so common and the abundant Sweet Chestnut that has been adopted as an honorary native.

Tree ID

NAME	DISTINGUISHING FEATURES

ASH ....
Bark: smooth, silvery green, more ridged in older tree
Seeds: single wing helicopters hang down in bunches known as 'keys', stay on tree through winter
Distinctive: black buds on bare branches in winter

BEECH ....
Bark: smooth, elephant grey bark, slumps round branches
Fruit: triangular nuts in spiky case known as beech masts
Distinctive: tight, pointed, upward curving buds in winter/early spring

BIRCH ....
Bark: papery, shiny peeling bark, coppery when young, silver/white older. Marked with distinctive black stripes where young branches have dropped
Flowers: brown droopy catkins April/May
Distinctive: large quantity of small twig drop around base of tree.

FIELD MAPLE ....
Bark: Orangey/brown ridges. Distinctive constrictions every 10–15cm in young tree branches.
Seeds: paired winged helicopters. Wings out to side like handlebar moustache

HAWTHORN (MAY) ....
Flowers: white froth of blossom in May, hence common name
Fruit: bright red berries in autumn
Distinctive: 1–2cm long thorns on twigs

HAZEL ....
Flowers: 3cm pale yellow dangling catkins early spring: February–March.
Fruit: small, hard-shelled nut. Papery case at base. Green turning to brown early autumn.
Distinctive: Often form multiple stems like shrub rather than single trunk.

HOLLY ....
Fruit: bright red berries in autumn and throughout winter in female trees

HORNBEAM ....
Bark: grey and smooth with vertical ridges
Flowers: Catkins May–June
Seeds: large winged bunches of keys in autumn
Easily confused with beech

HORSE CHESTNUT (CONKER) ...
Flowers: white pyramids known as candles
Fruit: distinctive inedible conker in spined green case

JUNIPER .... Fruit: blue/black berries tight to the twig in autumn

LARCH .... Leaves: needles in clumps go yellow in autumn and drop – not evergreen

OAK .... Bark: has deep chasms and ridges
Fruit: acorns in autumn
Distinctive: older trees are whiskery with short eruptions of twigs along big branches, often covered in moss and lichen.

ROWAN (MOUNTAIN ASH) ..... Bark: light grey and smooth
Seeds: bunches of bright orangey/red berries in autumn
Distinctive: often grow at higher altitudes or ornamentally at lower altitudes.

SCOTS PINE .... Bark: orangey/brown plates, ridged in old age
Distinctive: tree shape is typically tall, branchless trunk. Layered branches at canopy.

SWEET CHESTNUT .... Bark: brown ridges, often spiral to right up trunk.
Honorary native Fruit: edible nuts in autumn, brown nuts in green spiny sea urchin like case.

SYCAMORE .... Seeds: two seeded helicopters, Wings hang down like
Non-native 'biker' moustache.

WILD CHERRY .... Bark: bronze shiny bark which peels to reveal red underside, pocked with pores often set in lines around the trunk. Older tree cracks and flakes.
Flowers: white blossom in early spring.
Fruit: red cherries in autumn

GOAT WILLOW .... Bark: grey with diamond shaped pits.
Flowers: short stumpy catkin or pussy willow appears in early spring before leaves.

WILLOWS (WHITE/CRACK) ...... Bark: grey, rugged with criss-crossing ridges
Flowers: less distinctive longer dangling catkins
Distinctive: like damp or riverside conditions

YEW .... Bark: reddish brown with scales, beautiful grain on underside of flakes.
Fruit: red cup-shaped berries individually on twig in early autumn
Distinctive: native evergreen

Grow an oak

Wilderness Wood, East Sussex

... Today was Ruth's birthday and, as is becoming our tradition, we
went for a walk with our two dogs. Our friend Mireille came too and
on the way she told us about her oak tree. About ten years ago she was living in the
London suburbs, in a flat, surrounded by buildings and some way from the nearest
trees. One day, walking out on to her balcony, she glanced at her mop balanced upside
down and saw something nestling in amongst the damp strands. Closer inspection
revealed an acorn that had started to sprout. She was amazed and gazed around for a
while trying to work out how it had made its way to her mop. There was not a tree in
sight. Where had it come from and how did it get there? Maybe it was a sign, a gift
from heaven! She decided she had to plant it, so she found a pot and settled it in.
Since that day she has nurtured that miracle acorn which grew into a small seedling
and then an infant tree. She has moved four or five times and her oak tree has been
protected and lovingly transported from flat to house to flat. It has been afforded the
best spots on windowsills and in gardens. It has grown and been re-potted several
times and is now really beginning to look like a small tree. The mystery of how it
came to be in her regularly used mop will never be solved but it is a symbol of the
power of the oak over our emotions.

Usually an oak tree only starts producing acorns after around 30 years. Each year a
mature oak tree can produce around 2000 acorns and it has been calculated that an
acorn has a one in 10,000 chance of making it to a mature oak. If we consider that an
oak tree can live to be 1000 years old that is a potential of 194 offspring per oak tree.
The oak relies heavily on distribution by Jays that eat the acorns and carry them off
to bury them for winter supplies. Squirrels also do the same but it seems they are
much more heavy handed and few squirrel collections ever germinate as the acorns
are too bashed and bruised.

An emotional attachment to trees is not unusual and the oak seems to invoke
particularly strong emotions.

My mother-in-law recalls a visit to her grandparents as a child:

'I was about 10 years old, on a visit to my grandparents, when I was enchanted to see a row of plant pots on their living room windowsill, each with a 3 inch tall oak seedling. I do not know what had given my grandmother the idea to grow this little procession of trees. For several years afterwards it became my job to collect acorns in October or November for her to plant.

'I soon noticed that some of them had already begun to sprout, with a root emerging from the pointed end, luckily I sent them to her packed in damp moss; it seems acorns cannot survive drying even if they have not started to grow.

'I remembered all this years later, when I bought a Victorian glass acorn cup in a junk shop, I put an acorn in it and kept it by the sink so that I could easily keep it full of water. First the root grew long, winding round and round the glass, and then the shoot straightened out, growing to be about three inches tall with four to five leaves near the top. It kept me amused the whole winter.'...

How to grow an oak

If you want to grow your own oak tree from an acorn it is very straightforward but with no guarantee of success! Here's how to give it a go.

First go out and collect some acorns. The acorns you chose are probably the single most important factor on your quest to grow an oak. It is best to collect them in early autumn as soon after they have fallen as possible – oak trees shed their acorns in October. They should be brown and come away from the cup easily; the ones that have landed on a soft surface have a better chance of survival so collect those if you have a choice. If you find one that has already started shooting that is good. Check over your acorns carefully and discard any that have small holes where insects have got in or appear to have fungus on them. A good check of their viability is to put them into a bowl of water; if they float throw them away.

If you need to store your acorns before planting they must be kept moist and cool, away from direct sunlight. Pedunculate Oak (common or English oak) acorns do not need any pre-treatment to help them germinate, just keep them in damp conditions and they will begin to shoot.

Take the sinkers from the above float test and using my mother-in-law's technique put them on damp pea gravel in a bowl or suspend them above

feed to help its growth. It can take a while for the seedling to first appear – it may even be late spring – so be patient.

Once the seedling reaches 20cm tall it is ready to fend for itself. Find a spot where a 45m tree will have space and clear away all the vegetation and roots from a metre square. Dig a hole big enough for the roots and plant to the depth it was in its pot. Enjoy your oak tree, it could be there until your great, great, great, great, great, great, great, great, great, great, great, great, great, grandchildren are around.

some water in a hyacinth glass and keep them indoors so you can watch the growing process. If they are not already sprouting you will soon see a root emerging from the pointed end of the acorn. If kept indoors, a shoot will then emerge which will form four or five fresh green leaves that last for the whole winter and the following summer. You could plant them outside in the spring or keep them indoors until the autumn when the leaves will turn brown and fall off.

Alternatively, you can pot them out right from the start: two acorns in a seed pot or a yoghurt pot with drainage holes punched in the bottom. They should be covered with about 2cm of compost. The most important thing now is water. Keep them moist and in a shady spot – outside is best – they may need a mesh cover to keep away the mice. Water from above until the seedlings emerge. Once the leaves pop up you should start to water from below by standing your pot in a tray of water so the compost can soak it up through the drainage holes. In summer you can give it a light fertiliser

* The oak

The oak is the commonest tree in southern and central British broadleaf woodland. It is our national tree, the king of trees. The oak's dominance can in part be attributed to the value of its timber. Historically, most trees were coppiced and used for wood but oak timber was highly prized for construction and has been since prehistoric times. Oak trees, therefore, were not cut but nurtured and protected into maturity until they were large enough for use in ship building, construction and furniture making. In this way it has been given a competitive advantage over other woodland trees.

Oak not only had value as timber, the bark was used for tanning leather, the acorns are highly nutritious and were used as fodder for pigs, while branches and twigs were used for firewood and charcoal. Not only is the oak important economically but ecologically. The oak is well known for the diversity of its insect inhabitants. It is said that more than 400 different species of insect can live on the bark and leaves of one oak tree – much more than any other tree species.

Because of our long reliance on the oak it has become deeply embedded in our culture. Oak is invariably the tree of choice at tree planting ceremonies and the symbol of the oak leaf and acorn is used in logos by many businesses and nature trusts as it embodies the positive values of strength, longevity, reliability and environmental abundance.

Today the oak is under threat. Prior to 1900 oak in woodland propagated from acorns, however, since 1900 this behaviour has changed. Oaks have lost the ability to regenerate in woodland, and now only grow from seed out in the open (Rackham 2006). The most likely reason given for this change is an oak mildew from America that does not affect trees in the open but may be one challenge too far for an oak seedling struggling to grow in the shade of a wood. With no naturally grown oak seedlings since 1900 all woodland oaks today are mature trees of over 100 years old. Another threat to the oak is Acute Oak Decline. The extent and potential risk of this disease is unknown but currently under investigation. It is believed to be a bacterial infection that causes bleeding cankers on the oak's trunk.

Go nutty ... woodland forage

The Big Pitch, Norwich High School

... I used to play lacrosse at school and, for those of you uninitiated in the rules of lacrosse, there are actually no boundaries to a lacrosse pitch. It is at the referee's discretion as to when the players have gone too far and the game should be pulled back nearer to the centre circle. When I was at school we had the most beautiful line of beech trees down the side of our lacrosse pitch. It was usually understood that when play went beyond these beech trees you were off the pitch, however, in the autumn term it was quite feasible, while the play was down the other end of the pitch, to take a detour and wait for play to return at the side of the pitch and have a sneaky snack on the beech nuts ...

Foraging tips

WHEN TO FORAGE

Autumn is the best time of year for hungry woodland foragers. Along with the fungi popping up all over, the trees and bushes are all fruiting up with nuts and berries.

The edible nuts you may find in a good native woodland area are hazel nuts, beech nuts, sweet chestnuts and walnuts. Don't make the mistake of trying to eat horse chestnuts. However beautiful they look they do not taste good and are poisonous.

Complementing the nuts are the berries that begin to appear around this time of year: blackberries, elderberries, juniper berries, sloe berries, rosehips, wild raspberries, haws, and to go with them many of the cherry family (damsons and black cherries as well as the wild cherry) all bursting into fruit.

NUTS IN ORDER OF APPEARANCE

Walnuts Late August to September. A really productive wild tree is hard to find but if you get lucky you may find a treasure trove. The nut is encased in a green fleshy case called a hull which is very rich in tannins. Harvest from the ground or shake or knock the nuts out of the trees: you either need to wear gloves or accept dyed black hands from the tannins when you take the hulls off the shells which should come off easily if you have timed it right. The nuts then need to be left to dry out for a couple of weeks. You are then ready to sample them. Once cracked, eat immediately as the oils quickly become rancid when they are exposed to air. Those with cracked shells should be discarded.

Hazel nuts

Beech nuts

Hazel nuts Ripen late summer/early autumn from August to September. It is worth taking a sheet to put under the tree and give it a good shake to harvest a decent sized crop. You need to get in before the squirrels, as Squirrel Nutkin and his mates are efficient harvesters. Hazels taste beautiful straight from the green shell. We used to have hazels in our hedge and would spend hours cracking the shells with our back teeth to pull out the lovely sweet nuts. Straight off the tree they are crunchy, more like a bean or pea than a nut. When dried their shells turn brown and these are the ones we see in the nut bowl. Cobnuts are the cultivated hazel nuts you will find for sale at farmers' markets, much bigger than wild hazel nuts but still tasty.

Beech nuts Ripen in the autumn term between September and November. These small triangular nuts come in ones, twos or threes inside the beech mast. They are a high maintenance snack as you have to do battle with the spiky mast case before you get the triangular nuts out and even then you have to peel of one side of the nut case to get at the sweet nut inside. Because of the effort you have to make to access the nut I would suggest these are best for a snack as you stop for a rest under a beech tree rather than a major harvest. Either collect them from the ground or pick them straight from the tree as the mast begins to peel open.

Sweet Chestnuts Ripen from October onwards; they tend to come down with the leaves. Each hedgehog-spiked case will contain two to three plumply triangular shells – the plumper the shell the better the nut inside. While most nuts are protein-rich the chestnut is carbohydrate-rich and the groundnuts make great gluten free flour, used widely in France and Italy. They are excellent in a whole range of recipes but if you are foraging for them I think the best thing to do is to just slit the skin (so they don't explode) and

roast them over the fire. Peel off the skins and enjoy. To use them in cooking you would usually pour boiling water over the nuts. After they have soaked for a couple of minutes put them into cold water so they are cool enough to handle and then peel. It is quite a laborious job and the shell gets right in behind your thumbnail. It always brings back memories of Christmas as a child: we would spend hours peeling the chestnuts for our chestnut stuffing.

BERRIES AND FLOWERS

When it comes to nuts I find that the best way to enjoy nature's bounty is while you are out and about as you find them. I tend to forage for an instant snack rather than harvesting for major store cupboard supplies. However, for some of the berries it is a different matter. Berries can be found in great profusion and are easily picked for use in the kitchen so make easy rewards. Also, some of the berries can be a bit tart and are often better made into jams and jellies or used as flavourings in drinks.

Blackberries The harvest for British blackberries is between August and October, but mainly throughout September. They are a wonderful and common treat to sustain you on many a long walk. An organised picking expedition is always worthwhile as the berries taste great fresh, in crumbles and made into jams and jellies.

   Take plenty of containers, wear long sleeves and trousers to protect from the vicious bramble thorns and a walking stick to hook down the best, most juicy blackberries that are always found growing just out of reach.

Blackberries

Sloe berries From September onwards the purple black fruits of the blackthorn can be seen nestling in amongst the vicious branches of this hedgerow tree. They are well worth collecting. Although they are a little tart for fresh eating they make beautiful sloe gin and vodka, and can be used as an effective fabric dye, as well as in jellies and jams. To collect your sloes for gin

Sloes

Making elderflower cordial

making, it is traditional to wait until after the first frost. However, as long as they are not bullet-hard this is not too crucial. Collect your sloes carefully because the thorns of the blackthorn can make septic cuts that ache like no tomorrow.

To make sloe gin you need about 500g of sloes pricked or skins burst in some way. This is usually by pricking with a needle but I have heard that similar results can be obtained by putting them in the freezer and then defrosting. To the sloes add 250g sugar and cover with 1 litre of gin (vodka works equally well). Shake the mixture daily until all the sugar has dissolved and store in a cupboard for about three months. When the time is up strain out the sloes, bottle them up and wait for as long as you can bear. We usually manage until Christmas but I have been reliably informed that the longer you can wait the better it gets.

For an even simpler recipe, pick your sloes, freeze them overnight and then defrost. Half-fill a bottle with them and top it up with good quality gin (or vodka), leave for three months, strain and then add sugar syrup to get the right sweetness for your palate.

Juniper Juniper berries are an important constituent in the flavouring of gin but otherwise are generally used crushed or whole as a flavouring in casseroles or stews.

Elderflower The British summer is said to be heralded inwhen the elder flowers and summer is over when the berries ripen. Late May to June is a great time to pick the plates of fragrant misty white flower heads to make a summer cordial.

To make cordial collect 20–30 flower heads in a large bag or sheet. Leave them lying out head down for a while so that any wildlife can find its way out, otherwise you may find your kitchen full of bugs and beetles. Make a light syrup from a kilo of sugar in a litre of water by boiling the two together for a couple of minutes and then allow the syrup to cool. In a large bowl put the flower heads (cut as much of the stem off as possible at this point) and two sliced lemons. Pour over the cooled syrup. If you pour the syrup over while it is still hot your cordial will retain a strong element of the 'sweaty sock' basenotes that underlie the delicate champagne scent of the flowers. Leave the flowers to steep in the syrup for a couple of days in the fridge, stirring occasionally, then strain through muslin. Freeze the cordial in ice cube trays or a plastic container: the high sugar content will prevent it from going solid so you can scoop it out with a spoon straight from the freezer when you want a cool drink.

Put a spoonful with water, still or sparkling or a sparkling wine for a taste of summer. It can also be used to flavour jellies and ice cream for a special treat.

Some recipes suggest you include ascorbic acid (available from oriental supermarkets or chemists) as a preservative. With the addition of ascorbic acid the cordial will last a couple of months in a sterile, sealed bottle. Once open the cordial goes off quickly, even with the ascorbic acid, so must be used within a couple of days. I find it easier to omit the ascorbic acid and store in the freezer.

Elderberry The elder berries appear in early autumn. Elderberries contain a poisonous

Rosehips

alkaloid so they must be cooked to denature it before they can safely be eaten. Elderberries can be used in jams and jellies as well as crumbles and pies.

Damsons and cherry plums are great foraging fruits in late summer to early autumn. My grandmother's hedge has the most prolific supply of anywhere I have seen and we are always overwhelmed. This means crumbles every day, as many as you can eat, while you are collecting and jams and chutneys abound. You can even make a good damson gin or vodka in much the same way as you make sloe gin.

Rosehips As with sloes it is said that rosehips are best picked after the first frost. Generally from September onward pick them when they are at their brightest and plumpest and yield nicely to the touch. Rosehips are very high in vitamin C but beware the seeds that are coated in fine hairs: they are an irritant that was formally used

Elderberries

itching powder. To avoid the seeds, the best way to eat rosehips is to extract the juice. Throw them in a pan with some water and let them simmer away until they are pulped. Put through a muslin to separate the juice from the seeds and skins. The resultant juice can be boiled up with sugar – about equal quantities of sugar to juice – to make jelly or syrup that is great for warding off colds in the winter months. A short simmer will result in a syrup; the longer the simmer the thicker the syrup becomes until it reaches setting point and can be potted up for jelly.

Haws The beautiful red berries appear on the Hawthorn tree in autumn and are great for jellies and jams. As with rosehips, elderberries and sloes, extract the juice of haws by simmering the berries with a little water. Once fully pulped, strain through a muslin overnight. Add equal quantities of sugar to juice (1lb to 1 pint or 1kg to 1l). Add a little lemon juice or mix with apples for the pectin content to help with setting, boil up until the jelly reaches its setting point pot up and enjoy as an accompaniment to cheese and meats or just spread on bread and toast.

Haws

You don't need to buy flying toys, you just need to look in the woods. Many trees and other plants make use of the wind to disperse their seeds. The Ash, Sycamore, Elm, maple, fir, spruce and lime all produce seeds designed for wind dispersal.

Each tree produces its flying seeds in slightly different ways so if you find them on the ground amongst the leaf litter you can probably still identify which tree they come from, even if, as designed they have travelled some distance from the parent tree. There are several different names to describe these seeds: samaras, bracts or keys. They are also commonly known as helicopters, whirligigs and spinning jennies.

All sorts of seeds

Samaras   The sycamore and maple, coming from the same family, both have seeds known as samaras, they are two single nut-like seeds, each with a wing joined to one another. The Sycamore samara has two wings that join at about an angle of 120° rather like a very droopy Fu Manchu moustache. Maple samaras have a similar kind of helicopter with the two central seeds joined and wings that stick out sideways almost in a straight line, more like the classic handlebar moustache as seen extensively on heroic characters in First World War films and sported by Hercule Poirot.

Keys   The Ash seeds are known as 'keys'. They hang in bunches on the tree long into winter and can help with winter identification of the Ash tree. Each seed has a single wing that is much smoother to the touch and more symmetrical around the seed than either the maple or sycamore. They twirl to the ground rather than spinning.

Elm seeds

Bracts The Hornbeam has a very large, leaf-like, papery wing or bract fused to its single seed. It is trilobed with a large central finger and two smaller ones to either side. These bright green wings hang in clusters from the branches and spiral down from the tree after they ripen from September onwards.

The lime also has bracts, consisting of a single green, almost leaf-like, wing from which the paired seeds hang down on a long stem. You can distinguish between the large-leaved non-native lime and the native lime by the fact that the large leaved lime has more than two seeds per bract.

Elm seeds gather in pale but vibrant green translucent clusters. They appear on the tree before the leaves unfurl in early spring. Each seed is surrounded by a wafer thin but strong, circular papery disk, around 2cm in diameter.

Hidden seeds

The fir and spruce hide their seeds between the scales of their pinecones. They again vary in their shape and design but all based around the idea of a wing carrying a seed. Some look very like miniature individual ash keys, but only the size of a fingernail. Some look very much like a tiny manta ray with wide triangular wings and a thin tapering tail. The cones open up on dry days and the seeds are shaken out in a good wind to increase the chances of good dispersal. Squirrels also love a seedy snack and will munch their way through a pinecone in the same way as we would a corn on the cob, discarding the scales and guzzling the juicy fruit. This should also help with dispersal as the squirrel distributes the seeds as they pass through them.

Timing of seeds

The Ash, Sycamore, Hornbeam, Elm, lime and maple produce their winged seeds at different times throughout the year. The Elm is first in early spring followed by Ash keys which appear after the subtle purple flowers in May. They mature in August and turn brown on October but can be seen on the trees long after the leaves fall and often right through to the following spring. Lime bracts follow the yellow flowers in mid-summer. The Field Maple and Sycamore samara appear vibrantly green in late spring to early summer and mature in late September to October.

Make a moustache

In autumn it is often possible to find the brown remains of the helicopters nestled in amongst the leaf litter of the woods. The easiest to find are the sycamore and maple as the wing is robust and slower to decay than some of the other helicopters. Have fun wearing them as your favourite moustachioed character and then throw them in the air or launch them from a height and watch them twirl and spin down to the ground like a helicopter blade. See how far you can get them to fly, on a windy day they will sometimes be picked up on a breeze before they spin down to the ground some distance away.

Spot a fun guy

Banstead, Antique and Second Hand Book Fair

… There is a smell that envelops you as you leaf through an old book. An intoxicating perfume of dust and spores, dried leather and card. It has something of the woodland in it. Deep in the woods on a dry autumn day the same notes can be identified. For me the smell brings to mind green and brown tweed, leather elbow pads, relaxed armchairs. We've come to a secondhand book sale today and the smell forms a gentle 'curtain' as we enter the church hall. We chose an aisle each and begin to rummage, eyes scanning the spines picking out words and pictures to whet the appetite. Periodically we come together to share our treasures and then disperse again for further searching. Anousha has found a beautifully illustrated old copy of Cicely Mary Barker's *Flower Fairies*. We take it to the stallholder: £3000. It really was beautiful – a collector's item and more than a little beyond our budget. She searches on. Lottie is obsessed by a pocket-sized identification guide for mushrooms that is the perfect size for small hands. Eventually we buy this and a number of enticing looking stories and drag ourselves away from the musty treasures.

The mushroom book is an essential accompaniment to our walks from that day. We search out mushrooms and toadstools and do our best to identify them. There is a particular fascination in the ones marked 'poisonous' in bright red lettering with a black skull and crossbones …

Woodland fungi

Fungi grow in woodlands throughout the year but they become considerably more varied and abundant in autumn. The autumn of 2012 was a brilliant year for mushrooms and toadstools; every walk seemed to spring forth ever more brilliant and exotic forms growing in amongst the leaf litter, on living trees and on dead stumps and fallen trees. Fungi grow particularly well after a wet summer and 2012 broke many records for rainfall in the summer months.

Go for a walk and see how many different shapes and colours you can find. Where are they growing? Do they have stalks or gills? Take a picture or make a drawing and write down everything you think may be useful and then see if you can identify them. There are many books and websites you can employ when trying to identify mushrooms. The Field Studies Council foldout charts include a fungi name trail that is a great starting point for fungal ID in the woods.

Look out for the much-treasured Ceps (known as porcini in Italy) growing under conifers from July to November.

Every walk brings forth ever more brilliant and exotic forms of fungi, springing from trees, living and dead, and emerging in the leaf litter around their roots.

On sandy soils under birch or pine trees you may see the beautiful but highly poisonous Fly Agaric with its bright red and white spotted cap above snowy white stalk and white gills.

On birch trees you will often see infestations of the Birch Bracket or Birch Polyphore. Almost seeming to form steps up the side of the birch tree they are creamy brown and will eventually kill the tree.

Another tree killer is the Honey Fungus that has creamy gills that turn brown with age. It grows at the base of the tree.

One easily identified mushroom is the Puffball – the giant ones can look exactly like a football – almost as big and just sitting in the leaf litter as if discarded by a child. The Common Puffball is again white and round but smaller and with a chunky stalk and covered in small bumps.

Many of the fungi are named for the way they look – the name is almost just a description. Look for the Horse Hoof Fungus and the Ear Fungus – you will know them when you see them.

The Horse Hoof Fungus grows on many types of hardwood tree but typically on birch and beech. It is a parasite that enters the tree through a wound in the bark. It doesn't directly kill its host but may speed up its decline. It can live for years and once the tree dies, will act as a decomposer breaking down the dead timber. It is also known as the tinder fungus as it is great for making fires and will smoulder for hours. Chunks of the fungus were found on 5000-year-old Otzi the iceman and he was believed to be carrying them to use as a form of tinder.

The Ear Fungus grows on the dead branches of deciduous trees, particularly elder.

The vast majority of these mushrooms and toadstools do not look even slightly inviting as a snack and many are indeed poisonous. I am a complete novice when it comes to identifying mushrooms for eating so won't even begin to give you advice. If you are tempted to forage for mushrooms make sure you really know what you are doing. Several edible mushrooms have poisonous twins that can easily be confused. If you are in France you can take your mushroom haul to the pharmacist and they will be able to confirm which ones are edible for peace of mind. In this country, buy yourself a good mushroom identification guide and ideally go out with a mushroom expert a few times before you go it alone. Some of the most innocuous-looking mushrooms are the most toxic and they can be very variable in the field and notoriously hard to identify from a picture.

* Fungi

Fungi are extremely important to the woodland ecosystem, from microfungal symbiotic relationships in roots to parasitic mushrooms and saprophytic toadstools they all have their role to play in the life of the woodland.

Symbiosis is a mutually beneficial reliance or alliance between two organisms (in this case the fungus and the tree). A saprotroph is an organism (often fungus or bacterium) that feeds on dead and decaying organic matter. A parasite is an organism that feeds on living organisms (often but not always to their detriment). Fungi as a group use all these tactics to thrive in the woodland. They do not always stop at one tactic either. A fungus that may be parasitic and kill its host can then live saprophytically on the decaying tree.

The symbiotic relationship between micorrhizal fungi and tree roots is essential to the functioning of healthy woodlands. It is only in recent years that the importance of this relationship has been fully appreciated. Fungi form a micorrhizal association with over 80 per cent of the world's vascular plants. The fungus dramatically increases the area available for absorbing water and nutrients which it passes directly to the tree roots, in return the tree provides sugar-rich sap to the fungus from its photosynthetic production. The fungi form a whole network of micorrhiza linking the roots of different host species. This means that a woodland is a single functioning organism in an even more tangible way that the simple interactions and associations that us above ground dwellers can observe. Not all trees and vascular plants rely on this symbiotic relationship with the fungi to thrive.

Some parasitic fungi are very damaging to trees and can spread very rapidly. They have very light spores that are easily transported by water, wind, insects and man. Most fungi don't directly kill a healthy host tree. The Honey Fungus, for example, causes root and butt rot but will usually only kill the tree if it is compromised by other stresses such as excessive competition, drought or waterlogging.

Trees put up a lignified or tanninised barrier to fungal attack that prevents the spread of hyphae and looks like a black line – known as the R-zone. The fungus often add to the layer by producing a 'zone plate' when they reach the R-zone or a bit of tree inhabited by another fungus. The resultant wavy black line can be seen in the timber and is known as spalting. Spalted hardwoods produce a beautiful and distinctive timber much prized by furniture makers.

Ringwood Forest, New Forest, Hampshire

… My siblings and I have gathered together under the pretext of talking business but have managed to incorporate a large meal and two orienteering events. This morning we are deep in the New Forest jogging down woodland trails and heading off into the dense undergrowth with our highly coloured maps and compasses. The problem I always have is that for 11 months of the year I use OS maps to navigate my way round the country. Then my brother persuades me to do some

orienteering and they provide us with maps of indeterminate scale with all sorts of signs and symbols which mean very little to me. I know I have to find a check point in a green rhomboid and it says it is next to a small circle – I can't remember what a small circle means but it must be some kind of feature; maybe an unusual tree, a dip or a mound, I really can't remember. To further add to the confusion there are lots of people running around with maps but they are not necessarily doing the same course as me so it is folly to follow one of them, even though they clearly know exactly where they are going.

I get an immense sense of self-satisfaction every time I find a checkpoint but then immediately have to immerse myself back into the problem of finding the next one. Miraculously I keep finding the checkpoints and gradually my confidence is building so that I am able to raise my eyes from the map for more than a second at a time. Having achieved another checkpoint I come off a hill in the middle of the underbrush, see a path just where I expected it and head confidently down it at a good steady trot. 'About 200m down here and I should see a small track to the right …', 'that must be at . . . .

least 200m … no path' – I stop and scratch my head and peer around. The sun is in the wrong place, I look at the map, no I'm sure that is where I should be … gradually the incontrovertible truth of the sun's position sinks in and looking at the map I realise I came down the wrong side of the hill from the last checkpoint and am not on the path I anticipated. Feeling perversely pleased that I hadn't just continued blithely on, I retrace my steps and find the right path to eventually finish the course. A very satisfying event, great fun and I have definitely earned my rare breed hot dog from the caravan at the end …

Tips on navigating without maps

There are many clues you can use to help you navigate in the wild without resorting to maps and compasses. All you require is a basic knowledge of nature and your surroundings. You need to be alert and observant and some idea of where you have started and where you want to end up is also useful.

We all possess the basic skills of navigation but possibly haven't put them into a conscious framework. For example if you are on a walk and park at the top of the hill and head off downhill through a wood to a stream it is obvious that the route back to the car is not going to be following the stream downhill. At some point we must go back up a hill to return to our starting point – that is using common sense or a basic knowledge of the way the world works. If we were being observant on the route we would have noticed certain useful landmarks: benches, puddles or ponds, unusually shaped dead trees, moss covered logs, distinctive clumps of mushrooms or

flowers. These would all provide us with clues to use on the return journey and reassure us that we are on the right path. These observations are like the breadcrumbs that Hansel and Gretel laid on their route through the woods. If you make the right observations they will not change or disappear before you need them to find your way home.

The position of the sun, if it is not hiding behind too many clouds, is a great and reliable source of navigation as long as you remember it is moving. Knowledge about prevailing winds and the behaviour of plants and animals can also help with navigation.

The prevailing wind in the UK is from the south-west so sideways leaning trees in exposed positions are a particularly clear indication of the direction of the prevailing wind. Within a woodland these effects are harder to see but trees will still often fall in high winds, even if they were killed by disease. The final straw is often a high wind and they will therefore typically lie in a south-west–north-east orientation.

Growth patterns Even in life a tree will give away the direction of the prevailing wind by its growth patterns. Prevailing winds from a consistent direction will cause extra wood to be laid down to counteract the force as a tree grows. It is important to know, that conifers will lay down the extra wood on the leeward side of the trunk and broadleaved trees lay down the extra wood on the windward side of the trunk. (The same is true of branches. A conifer will support its branches by building up its support on the

underside while broadleaves will support the branch with extra wood on the upper side.) So look for a broader trunk on the north-eastern side of conifers and on the south-westerly side of broadleaved trees.

Moss and lichen are often quoted as growing on the north side of trees but this not a reliable guide. Their growth relies on many factors including the texture of the bark, availability of sunlight and water. Lichens are very variable and different species thrive in different conditions. You will see whole stands of trees sporting one side coloured by a particular lichen species and that may help you to identify a route home but whether it is on the north side or south depends heavily on the local conditions and the individual species. A good supply of water is most important for mosses and they tend to grow in the crooks of branches and around tree bases, however, there may be more growth on the north side that is away from the sunlight and dries out slower.

Route-finding games

The more observant you are as you walk the greater your chances of finding your way. There are some games you can play to test your skills of observation and navigation.

HANSEL AND GRETEL GAME

This game can be particularly fun if you are in an unfamiliar wood with someone who knows it quite well. Ask someone to lead you on a trail through the woods. Then, see if you can find your way back to the starting point. Only go quite small distances to start with, then extend them as you grow in confidence.

Use all your senses to identify the path but make sure you are noting permanent, unchanging clues. It is no good relying on the knocking of a woodpecker that may fly off but noting the direction of the sound of flowing water may be useful. However that will not be enough on its own, you need to build up the full picture of your route. Like breadcrumbs scattered along the path, make a trail of observations that will help you find your way home. See how long and complicated the trail can be before you become confused and can't find your way.

ROUTE SONGS

Another game to play using your powers of observation is to make a route song. The aboriginal peoples of Australia sing their way across their territories using songlines that are handed down through the generations. These songs identify landscape features set into stories and dances from the dreamtime that enable them to travel vast distances without getting lost.

From a known starting point, each person takes a route through the woods to a recognisable end point. This end point may be a distinctive natural feature such as a rock, tree stump, river pool or it could be something you have put there yourself – a jumper or backpack or some treasure – food treats or similar.

Then each person makes up a song that describes in detail their route from the starting point to the treasure.

You can make up your own music or set it to a clapped rhythm or rap or to the tune of a known song. Once each person has perfected their route song meet up again at the starting point and teach each other the route song. If you are a large group it is probably best to teach the song to just one other person. You should then attempt to follow each route song to see if you can actually reclaim the treasure or find each end point. This could be done in pairs and over quite short distances if there are very young children involved to make sure no one gets lost.

Using your own landscape knowledge is a lot of fun and counteracts our reliance on maps and satnavs that have stripped out most of the interesting features in our path. In the past directions were so much more fun: 'head down the hill into to town, over the level crossing, turn left at the playground past the Chequers Pub, in a mile or so you'll see a big old oak tree take the first right past that and the house is three doors down from the phone box by the duck pond'. These days we just ask for the postcode, plug it into the satnav and head off blindly, looking at a screen that shows just the road and road names but no features at all.

* Mosses and lichens

Mosses and lichens are epiphytic which means they rely on the tree as a surface to grow on but they take their nutrients from the air and rain not from the tree itself. They are not parasitic and don't cause any damage to the host tree.

LICHENS There are around 1800 species of lichen identified and living in the British Isles at present, roughly similar to the sum of all native vascular plant species, but the list keeps getting longer (BritishLichens.co.uk).

Lichens are actually a symbiotic partnership of a fungus and either a green alga (photosynthetic) or cyanobacteria (nitrogen fixing), sometimes both. They have developed their life form to enable them to inhabit a wide range of habitats, often where lack of water or nutrients means few other species can survive. They can withstand

long periods of desiccation when they dry out and enter a kind of stasis; as soon as water becomes available they bounce back. Our temperate woodland environments are not extreme but the lichens cling to surfaces that few other plants could survive on. Some of our lichens are very sensitive to changing environmental conditions and their presence or absence can tell scientists much about the prevailing air quality.

Lichens share some similarities with corals and display almost as many different morphologies and colours. The many different growth forms may be described as:

leafy – foliose

crusty and flat – crustose

shrubby – fruticose

scaly – squamulose (britishlichens.co.uk)

It is the species of fungus that dictates the morphology of the lichen although it cannot grow into that shape without the algae. Some fungi will have a different form when associated with cyanobacteria from the same fungus with an alga.

Historically lichens have been used as food, for dyes and early antibiotics. They are also used in modelling, My brothers used to make papier mâché terrain for their toy soldiers to fight on and the toy shop sold clumps of lichens as miniature trees and shrubs.

MOSSES Mosses have no water transport system and no waterproofing to prevent the loss of water and therefore require damp conditions in which to grow. Because of this they favour trees with a rough bark that retains sufficient water for them to become established and they have developed a sponge-like morphology that allows them to trap water in amongst their leaves and stems to make the most of the water available.

When they can get enough moisture, mosses form luxuriant, vibrant green carpets and mats on trees. These are typically around the base of trees, giving the impression that the trees are wearing rather lurid leg warmers, or at the junction of branches and on the upper surfaces of large branches. Mosses are never parasitic – they don't root properly into the tree but just grip the surface with rhizoids. Different species are associated with different tree species. A broadleaf moss will not grow on or under a conifer and vice versa. Some species are able to go into a dormant phase if they do dry out and can then rehydrate when conditions are favourable however most do not and unlike the lichens they are typically susceptible to desiccation.

The spongy, moisture retaining properties of mosses were utilised historically as a packing material for transporting goods, particularly those that would need to be kept damp such as plants and seeds. Their absorbent and mildly antiseptic properties were exploited in their use as nappies and as wound dressings in the First World War.

What's in the woods?

Clifton's Lane, North Downs, Surrey ... January

... This morning I went for a run along a path heading up onto the North Downs. I probably walk, cycle or run up this path three times a week and I often see other people with dogs, horses and bicycles. Many birds from the surrounding trees dart across the path and occasionally I have seen deer dashing off into the undergrowth but I have rarely seen any other wildlife. Leading up through an avenue of trees, the stony, muddy track is usually bumpy and sometimes churned to mud by the regular foot and cycle traffic of an averagely busy bridleway. However, last night we had quite a significant fall of snow. The trees are hanging low with their white burden and the ground has lost all its definition lying silently under its sparkling, sugar-encrusted, whipped-cream blanket. The path under the shelter of the trees only has a couple of inches of cover but in its smooth surface I can see the tracks of every man and beast who has passed this way since the small hours of the morning, when the snow stopped falling. It is fascinating to see with whom I share this path and presumably do every day. The entire way up the track I follow the bear-like five clawed marks of a Badger. Criss-crossing the path are Rabbit tracks that always remind me of Munch's painting 'The Scream' and deer prints, along with numerous bird prints of all shapes and sizes. I can even make out the feather prints of a Pheasant's wing where it has apparently taken flight. Alongside these are mountain bike tracks, horses' hoof prints, several large booted humans and a smattering of dogs. It is lovely to see some evidence of animals going about their lives all around us without our even knowing it ...

How to work out what's in the woods

Sometimes the woods can feel quiet and lonely. Walking down a path that winds its way through the cool greenery, aside from the occasional chirp of a bird as the light filters down from the tree canopy, we remain blissfully unaware of the wildlife that has been active around our feet before and after our passing.

There are many little clues we can find when we look closely at our surroundings to see the animals we are sharing our woodland with. It is often surprising and very illuminating. Snow is a great opportunity to get a snapshot view of animals' behaviour; you can also see footprints in mud patches and sandy areas. Go for a walk and look out for other signs to tell you which animals frequent the woods. Have a look for

marks and damage on tree trunks and branches. Have a rummage under a nut tree – nibbled nutshells give away a lot and can tell you which animals have been feeding there. Entrances to dens, setts and warrens all identify their owner.

BARK DAMAGE

Many small and large mammals like to chew on tree bark, particularly the soft juicy bark of a young sapling. So have a look at the bark on trunks and branches to see what has been having a nibble. The height of the damage and the edge of the cut both indicate of the culprit.

Deer damage is the highest up the trunk at 1–1.8m. Deer, like sheep have no front teeth in their upper jaw so they will leave a jagged edge to the bark they strip off. Young male Roe Deer – roebucks – scrape their new-grown antlers on trees to remove the velvet coating – known as fraying, this often leave scrapes on the bark or even shredded ribbons of bark hanging off the trees – it literally frays the bark.

Hares can reach up to about 70cm and Rabbits up to 50cm and they often nip the top off saplings or take the ends off branches. Hares are more sporadic in their attacks but can take out a whole row of trees once they get started. Rabbits and hares along with the voles and mice have sharp teeth and leave a sharp cut edge when they eat as if cut by a knife.

Voles often nibble away at the very base of the tree – they may ring bark up to 10cm from the ground while dormice and squirrels climb trees and chew away at the base of branches.

Domestic animals such as horses and sheep can be a real problem for trees and are usually kept away. Trees alongside horse fields are often extremely gnarled, if they manage to survive, as a result of the constant chewing on their bark.

Even if the tree is not killed directly by grazing it can still cause a problem. Any bark damage is a potential route in for fungi and other disease organisms that may weaken and ultimately destroy the tree.

FOOD REMAINS

Squirrels love the seeds of conifers and will shred and nibble away at the scales of pinecones to get at the nut-like seeds sandwiched between them. You will often see the remains of cones with just the top two or three scales left while the rest have been stripped away.

Hazel nuts give great clues as to who has been nibbling them. A nut eaten by a dormouse will have a smooth circular hole that often crosses the nut scar and there will be gnaw marks around the hole. The Bank Vole's nut has a chiselled inner edge to the circular hole but without the gnaw marks and not crossing the nut scar. The Wood Mouse makes a chiselled hole with gnaw marks and not crossing the nut scar. A nut eaten by a squirrel will be split in two, top to bottom if eaten by an adult or broken into with a jagged edge by a younger animal.

DENS AND HOLES

If you find a den you can check whether it is a Badger's sett, Fox's earth or Rabbit's burrow by having a good look round the hole.

A Badger's sett will have several entrance holes in one place; they are usually dome-shaped and 25–30cm in diameter, larger in sandy soils. They invariably have a large heap of spoil outside and look out for black and while hairs caught on

brambles or other vegetation nearby. Fox earths are usually solitary, taller than they are wide and only 20–25cm diameter. Thre may be a musty smell and the excavated soils form a fan shape in front of the earth. Rabbit burrows are smaller, 10–20cm – usually with lots of droppings outside and several entrances to a large warren system around and about.

You can check whether the holes are still in use without waiting around for ages by gently placing crossed twigs over the hole, if they have been pushed away by your next visit it could well be an active hole.

You may even see some evidence of Wild Boar as you wander round the woodlands of south-east England. It is estimated there may be between 500 and 1000 Wild Boar in the woodlands of, mostly, southern England; they are largely offspring of escapees from boar farms and wildlife parks.

Night walking

Amazon rainforest, Ecuador

... On our honeymoon Dunc and I visited the Amazon rainforest as part of a group. We slept in thatched huts at night sheathed in sleeping bags and mosquito nets in individual bunks. As we prepared for bed and lay in our bunks the roof of the hut was dotted with a constellation of paired 'stars' – a myriad of spiders that fed and nested in the warm thatch.

At the end of a day, when we had come across a tarantula which our guide had placed on Dunc's back and allowed to climb up on to his head, the 'stars' in the thatch swam and blurred as I drifted off to sleep. In a vivid dream I became convinced that I had a tarantula in my mosquito net and woke wide-eyed, my heart pounding deeply. I couldn't tell if I had my eyes open or closed as it was pitch black.

A little flustered I asked Dunc to pass me a torch so I could investigate. He, drowsy and cosily tucked up, told me there really wasn't a problem and I should just go back to sleep. Getting more and more agitated I asked with increasing volume and intensity for him to get me a torch and started thrashing around tangling myself in net and sleeping bag. He calmly tried to reassure me that there wasn't a spider in my bag and that I should just settle down and go back to sleep. The situation was only resolved when a weary fellow traveller suggested Dunc should, 'just get her a torch mate, then we can all get back to sleep'. I made a thorough investigation of every inch of my bed, sleeping bag, rolled clothes pillow and mosquito net and found not so much as a money spider. I diligently straightened all my tangled bedding out and tightly re-tucked my mosquito net ensuring there were no gaps or holes and finally turned off the torch allowing everyone to get back to sleep ...

Experience the woods at night

The woods at night are a very special place. More than anything I love to immerse myself in the darkness, to stop and melt into a tree trunk and be invisible. That is when you can 'see' the most. Without the distraction of sight you can focus on the sounds. Different woods have different sounds that will also change with the seasons. Just by virtue of different species and different management techniques the wind in the canopy will sound quite different. Sleeping in a Sweet Chestnut coppice in summer the wind in the highly mobile canopy sounded like the hissing of small waves on a sandy beach, in winter the same woodland lost the beach-scape but became a haunted house characterised by the tapping, creaking and squeaks of overlapping limbs knocking and rubbing against each other.

TAKE A TORCH

I tend to have a running battle with my companions when I am out at night. I like to allow my eyes to adjust to the dark and would rather travel slowly, stumbling over tree roots and feeling my way through the tree trunks than to use a torch. Most other people I find like to have a torch and see where they are going. Nevertheless, I do concur that torches do enable you to get out and be active when eyesight is not up to the job; using maps, pitching tents and running or cycling on tracks are hard to do without some help. I have also found that torches can also be surprisingly great for wildlife spotting.

Perceived wisdom tells us that to spot wildlife you should make yourself as inconspicuous as

possible. You should camouflage yourself and sit very still and any lighting should be infrared night vision goggles. This is true if you want to photograph wildlife or to watch Badgers or other wildlife for an extended viewing. However, some of my best wildlife 'spots' have been through the use of a torch. The technique is to keep the beam moving, rather like a sport fisherman casting a fly, cast the beam around you. Look at ground level as well as up in the tree canopy. I can almost guarantee that before long you will capture in your beam the reflected paired beams of an animal's eyes. The great thing about hunting for eyeshine is that you will spot animals quite some distance away and often where they would otherwise be concealed by leaves or undergrowth.

HOW ANIMALS SEE IN THE DARK

Most nocturnal animals (and deep sea animals) have a reflective membrane at the back of their eye behind the rods and cones of the retina – the *tapetum lucidum* (or bright tapestry). The purpose of the membrane is to reflect back light through the eye, allowing the available light to be used twice, giving better vision in low light conditions. Although animals are unlikely to hang around in a torch light they can be visible from some way off by the glow of their eyes. The colour of the reflected light varies between animals and apparently with different light levels. To help identify the animal you have captured the usual colours are: red in owls, Nightjars and rodents, pale blue in deer, sheep, cows and horses and green in Foxes, cats and dogs. Spiders' eyes are yellow – exactly like paired stars!

* Badger (Meles meles)

The sight of a black-and-white snout poking out of its hole sniffing in the night air, followed by the distinctive striped face and bumbling, round back and bottom is something you will never forget. If you want to watch Badgers probably the best place to start is to go on an organised Badger watching adventure. Local wildlife trusts often run these kinds of events.

If you have identified a Badger's sett and want to watch out for its owner, find a comfortable position out of the way downwind of the sett and sit very quietly. Badgers don't have the best eyesight but they do have great hearing and sense of smell. As Badgers are nocturnal, settle down to watch at dusk to get the best chance of seeing them in action.

Badgers live in social groups of between four and 12 individuals; the females are called sows and the males, boars. They typically mate in spring but due to a long stage before the embryo implants, the young are not born until the following February. A litter consists of between one and four cubs but usually two or three. The young feed on their mother's milk until they are four months old when they move on to an omnivorous diet like their parents. Badgers will dig around for their food and eat anything from beetles, rodents, wasp larvae and frogs to cereals, nuts, seeds and berries. Probably their most important food source is earthworms.

Badgers are very strong diggers, in fact their name comes from the French 'becheur' meaning digger. They dig out extensive burrow systems that are used from generation to generation; some are thought to be centuries old. These setts have numerous chambers that they keep scrupulously clean, pulling out and replacing the bedding regularly to prevent infestations with lice and tics. They use a 'latrine' outside the sett to help keep it clean.

Badgers have been persecuted by humans in the 'sport' of Badger baiting where people pit dogs against the Badger and bet on the outcome. The fights are very vicious with dogs and Badgers often being horrendously injured. Badgers sometimes even have their feet or tails nailed to the floor to even up the fight. Badgers are protected by law but in 2013 they were subject to culling in certain areas in a controversial attempt to control TB in cattle.

* Common Dormouse
(Muscardinus avellanarius)

The Common or Hazel Dormouse is small (8cm long body), shy, nocturnal and rare so the chances of seeing one in the wild are very low; you also need a licence to handle them. It is the only British mammal other than bats that hibernates. They hibernate from October to May.

The dormouse lives and feeds in particular on hazel and honeysuckle although it will take many other flowers nuts and fruit. As a particular delicacy the dormouse eats the larvae of the gall wasp as we would do biscuits. The gall wasp lays its larvae on the leaves of oak so the dormouse is a big help to the oak tree in clearing the larvae. Later in the season they then move onto blackberries and hazelnuts, fattening themselves up for six months of no food as they hibernate.

The dormouse has a reputation for sleepiness as we all know from the Mad Hatter's Tea Party in *Alice in Wonderland*. They are typically sluggish during daylight hours and hibernate for six to eight months of the year, depending on temperatures. They hibernate underground using moss and honeysuckle bark to line their nests. As they hibernate their body temp drops to that of the surroundings and their heart rate to a tenth of its rate when awake.

The dormouse lives at a completely different scale to us. Its tiny size allows it to run around in the tree canopy from tiny twig to leaf without danger. Even if it falls from that great height it is so light that it is unharmed: it just jumps up and scuttle off. But their small size also requires the heart to beat at a much faster rate than ours and consequently they live much shorter lives.

Abinger Common, Surrey

... We were tree climbing today at Abinger Common. It was a beautiful megalith of a beech tree. Not that old but my goodness it was tall. Standing on the side of a gentle slope we used a stick to estimate the height that Dunc climbed to at about 30m and there was more above that. Beech are lovely to climb as they have such clean branches, the bark is not too aggressive so your skin and clothes don't get too shredded and the branches stay a good diameter right through the body of the tree. They are strong enough that you feel confident they are going to take your weight but they are not so thick that it is hard to climb them. This particular beech tree demonstrated a particularly rich variety of natural grafts. Almost every step of the way branches had overlapped and bound themselves together, the bark wrapping around the two branches and hugging them together in a display of over-enthusiastic growth. I've never seen so much on one tree ...

What are natural grafts?

It is not unusual to come across wild trees whose branches or even trunks have formed natural grafts where the branches or trunks appear to have grown together and merged to form one stem. This is exactly what happens, as the bark of the two stems rub together the bark wears away on each flank until the cambium is exposed. Once the cambium of the two trees touches it grows together so that they are nourishing each other and sharing sap. The bark cambium from each limb goes into overtime and wraps around the conjoined cambium, forming a graft between the two limbs.

This grafting process is known as inosculation. These limbs may be from one tree or from neighbouring trees; they are not necessarily even from the same species (although different species generally are not true grafts of the cambium). If you see a cut cross section of a tree

at the point that it has grafted, it is quite fascinating. There are two centres like a double crown in a head of hair, the two sets of rings at head out concentrically from their centres until the point where the cambium joined. The next layer of wood wraps around the whole combined stem in a figure of eight pattern, each layer expands on this becoming an ever widening hourglass shape until it gradually fills out to an oval. There is sometimes even a small section of bark captured in the centre of the tree.

Pleaching and inosculation

The ability of trees to inosculate is exploited in agriculture and garden design. Pleaching is a technique often used by farmers to weave together the stems of trees to form stock-proof hedges. It has been adopted widely in garden design as it provides a good screen and can create arches and arbours. Where the woven branches and stems overlap, they will often graft together to form an impenetrable bond, great for stock control and beautiful too.

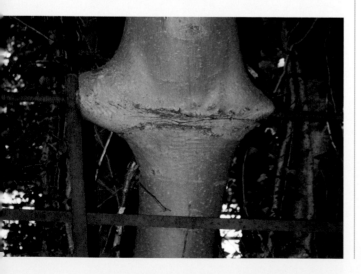

As a child I had a book of 'tricks to stun and amaze your friends'. One was to put a ring or quoit on a branch and then bind the branch with another below the ring so that you would end up with a ring stuck on the tree. I never tried this but I'm always thinking about it. Roger Deakin and David Nash have both used pleaching and inosculation on their tree manipulations. Both made Ash arbours with bound ash boughs growing together and forming a natural arch. Thin barked trees are the most likely to show natural grafts, particularly fruit and nut trees, Ash and beech as well as Blackthorns and willows.

Avoiding obstacles

Trees can grow around anything that gets in their way. There are many examples where trees have been subject to man's interference and overcome it. Trees in hedgerows or woodland boundaries often have barbed wire or metal fences embedded deep in their trunk. And dramatically-shaped tree trunks may form to avoid hazards or barriers. Some tree artists have exploited this ability of trees by training the tree to grown in a particular shape. Check out the work of Richard Reames of Arborsmith (www. arborsmith.com) and Peter Cook of Pooktre (www.pooktre.com) to see amazing living tree designs.

Go for a walk in the woods and you may not see any tree chairs but you will see some great natural tree formations, and before long you will be spotting natural grafts all over the place. See how many different varieties and examples of living tree sculpture, scarring, **pleaching and inosculation you can find.**

Woodland adventures come in all shapes and sizes. It is all in the state of mind: think big or think small but think adventurously. Here are some ideas for engaging with the woodland environment in an active way.

Climb into the canopy

Headley Heath, Surrey

... The oak tree looks down from the crest of the sandy slope, its shaggy head inclined, two solid, moss laden arms outstretched, just asking to be climbed. When you place one hand on the shoulder of each of the two big side branches this beautiful old oak draws you into its centre. I can just reach a foot up into the crook the branches create with the trunk and lever myself up into the tree. From here the branches spiral out from the centre line so that I feel nicely enveloped as I continue to reach higher and higher into the tree. Without ever feeling exposed I can reach well up into the tree and perch like an oversized owl on a branch and peer around over 360 degrees of woodland and heath. Alfie sits patiently at the bottom of the tree once he has decided I may be some time and I am free to investigate the amazing array of greenery that is hitching a ride on the rough bark of the oak. It is no surprise that the oak is so valued in conservation for its number of associated species: every limb is its own scaled down rainforest rich in micro-niches and supporting its own miniature woodland of plants and animals ...

How to climb into the canopy

Not all trees are conveniently shaped for climbing, particularly in woodland where the trees use their energy in growing tall and straight, to find sunlight, before they start to add side branches. Nevertheless, if you hunt them out they can be found. Dotted throughout most mixed woodland, suitable shaped yews, oaks and beeches, particularly on the margins of woodlands and in clearings, are worth hunting out and many smaller trees also provide a very satisfying climb.

As you are climbing be constantly aware of the integrity of the branches to which you will be trusting your weight. As a rule of thumb any branch wider than your wrist should be strong enough to hold your weight. Keep a careful eye

out for dead branches and avoid them. In winter it can be hard to work out which branches are dead or alive, if you are unsure chose another branch or stand close to the junction with the main trunk and you should be fine.

It is not always the giants of the tree world that provide the best tree climbing experiences. Some of the smaller trees will bend under your weight but they are more than springy enough to return to their starting point – birch and alder are particularly good for this and provide a unique climbing experience. Robert MacFarlane recounts climbing birches in the Lake District that bent so much he was able to step off the top of the tree onto the hillside whereupon the tree sprung back to its original position.

Up in the tree you may feel more confident in a good solid oak that barely moves but a more mobile birch or alder that sways in the wind and as you move around really makes you feel a part of the living world.

When you are up in your tree you are really in another world. Face to face with the tree and all that it experiences you can see the world below from a new perspective. Often when up in a tree I see people walk past below, yet they rarely look upwards and see me: I can observe the world of the woodland as it goes on all around me. The wildlife in the canopy seems surprisingly unconcerned by my presence and the world on the ground is entirely unaware of my existence; I am invisible. It is a wonderful treat to be able to experience our world from a new dimension and to feel entirely immersed in the canopy of the woods.

If you don't feel confident climbing trees on your own then there are other ways you can get

Recreational tree climbing

I have always wanted to get up into the tree canopy. For years I have been enthralled by the work of biologists in the Amazon rainforest and have dreamed of sitting in a tree high above the forest floor surrounded by branches and the leaves, head in the clouds with the birds flying around me. Obviously I have talked about this so much that eventually my husband acted on it for my birthday. No, not a holiday in the Amazon but a canopy access course. As a child I was always accused of behaving like a monkey and spending all my time upside down. Well for two days, all of us learned to be professional monkeys.

Using the techniques employed by tree surgeons, our instructor Roland, from the recreational climbing company Treefrog, spent a couple of days teaching us all the rope skills we would need to be able to climb safely into the tree canopy.

We are now able to climb up previously inaccessible trees right up into the canopy, swing from tree to tree, walk out on branches, sling hammocks and generally hang out. For my husband, who craves rock faces, it is the closest he has found in the southern lowlands to replace the call of the rock. For me it is the key to another world. Quite often I can be up a tree right next to a path and people won't even know I am there – in the parallel universe of the canopy.

into the canopy. There are several places you can walk or climb up to the tree canopy on ladders and walkways, for example The Royal Botanical Gardens in Kew and Salcey Forest in Northamptonshire. There are a whole rash of rope adventure courses throughout the country run by companies such as Go Ape, High Ropes and others and there are even several recreational tree climbing companies who will teach you how to climb trees yourselves.

Make mega swings

If some trees are crying out to be climbed then some branches emerge at such an inviting angle that you just have to sling a rope over for a swing. Mega swings need a high branch to hang a rope from. The higher the branch you sling your rope over, the better the swing. A long rope swing swings slow, and long, the wind your hair is gentle and the long trajectory of the pendulum means you really have the sensation that you are flying.

We use a harness and tie in to the bottom of the rope swing which makes it very safe for small children. If you are making mega swings without a harness make sure that people are strong enough and sensible enough to hold onto the swing until they have their feet firmly back on solid ground

How to get a rope over a high branch

Getting the rope over the branch is often the hardest part of setting up a rope swing. On our tree-climbing course we used two techniques both of which require you to throw something

Safety tips

● MAKE SURE YOUR BRANCH IS SOUND – IT IS HARD TO MAKE A CLOSE EXAMINATION OF A BRANCH HIGH IN A TREE SO TEST THE BRANCH FOR STRENGTH BY BOUNCING ON THE SWING A FEW TIMES BEFORE YOU LAUNCH ANY SMALL CHILDREN OFF.

● MAKE SURE YOUR ROPE IS COMPLETELY SOUND – IT SHOULD BE AT LEAST 10MM DIAMETER WITH NO VISIBLE DAMAGE – FRAYING OR CUTS ARE DEFINITE NO-NOS.

● MAKE SURE THE ROPE IS NOT HANGING OUT OVER SPACE WHEN IT COMES TO REST. IF IT IS THEN YOU WILL NEED TO DEVISE A WAY TO PULL THE SWINGER BACK IN OR THEY MAY GET STRANDED.

● IF YOU ARE NOT USING HARNESSES MAKE SURE YOUR SWINGER IS CAPABLE AND SENSIBLE ENOUGH TO HOLD ONTO THE ROPE FIRMLY FOR THE LENGTH OF THE SWING.

● REMEMBER YOU ARE RESPONSIBLE FOR ANYONE WHO GOES ON YOUR SWING. IF YOU HAVE ANY DOUBTS ABOUT SAFETY, DON'T DO IT.

over the branch and Roland will confirm that this is not my best skill but it is definitely a case of practice makes perfect and I'm improving.

FOR BRANCHES UP TO 5M

The first technique is just to manually throw your rope over the branch. With this technique you make a 'monkey' with the end of your rope to give you something heavy to throw. If you tie it correctly it will untie as it goes over the branch and the end will be long enough to reach you back down on the ground again.

To make a 'monkey' wind a few short coils of rope over your hand. Then wrap, just below your hand, with a couple of turns of the rope and push a bight of rope through the top of the coil. Hold the bight of rope with the top of the coil. You don't tie any knots in this system.

To throw the 'monkey', hold onto the top of the coils and the bight you pushed through. Make sure the length of rope on the ground is free to move, then swing with a straight arm to throw the monkey over the branch. As it clears the branch the bight will slide out of the coils and the rope will unravel as it returns to the ground.

Vary the number of coils in the monkey to ensure the rope reaches back down to the ground once it has flown over the branch. This is a very simple system that can be used for branches up to 5 metres off the ground or a bit more if you are very good.

FOR BRANCHES OVER 5M

For this height you will need a throw line and throw bag. The throw line is any fine string or cord and you can buy throw bags but they can also be easily made. To make a throw bag put a tennis ball or cup of sand in a sock, tie up the neck and ideally tie a ring to the neck of the bag to help with the throwing technique described below. Tie the thin string onto the 'bag' ensuring the string is long enough to go over the branch and back down to the ground again.

The next challenge is to launch your bag over the branch. There are many different ways to pitch a throw line and I haven't perfected any of them. Probably the most successful and simple is to push a loop of string through the ring of the bag and allow the bag to hang down between your legs holding the top of the loop in one hand

Making a 'monkey'

and the same length of string in the other. Make sure your string is free to run out. Stand with your back to the branch you are aiming for and look up at it – if you are in the right position you should be able to see it without hurting your back. Swing the bag back and forth with straight arms at shin height and then swing the bag up until your arms are above your head. At the highest point let go, hopefully launching it up and over the branch. You may not be successful first go but keep practising and you may get really good. Some people prefer to use the same technique but throw facing the branch so you could give that a go as well.

Once you have your throw line over the branch and the bag is back down to earth attach the rope to the cord and pull it up and over the branch.

Cammas an Eilan, Ardeishlaig Peninsular, Scotland

... We are staying on a small peninsular on the west coast of Scotland for a few days. When I was a child we used to come up here for our summer holidays and camp on some rough land belonging to my mother's friend. Years later we discovered that a university friend has a house on the next outcrop along down the shore from our former campsite and so we have come to stay. The house is entirely on its own on a wooded rock sticking out into the sea loch. At night we can see the lights dotted along the shoreline and mirrored in the inky water indicating where the neighbours are. The house is well supplied with bicycles and kayaks, chopped wood and its own resident Pine Marten. And perhaps best of all, in amongst the trees they have slung a vast fishing net. At about 5 metres square it is stretched horizontally between a metre and two metres off the ground. It is fantastic. We can clamber around in it like a horizontal cargo net, which is amazingly hard work. We have found it is great for games of 'it' and chasing a ball around in a deranged version of handball. It is also lovely to just hang out in, eating snacks and reading books and looking up into the canopy; like being in a giant hammock ...

How to hang out in trees

There are many ways you can spend time in trees and the longer you can hang out the more you can commune with the woods.

If you climb a tree it is not long before the branches start digging in and you need to move or descend. You need to find some way to make your perch in the tree more comfortable to enable you to hang out longer.

Hammocks are a great way to be able to do this and hang nets are an even better alternative for communal living. Another alternative, available in all woodlands is a tree house.

Every childhood should incorporate some kind of tree house. The best in my opinion are just dens that have moved up the tree. The hardest part of a tree house is finding the perfect perch. The junction between large branches is the best location and they also need to be accessible.

Once you have found a good spot in the branches of a tree, the same materials that you would use for den building can be employed. The most important elements are good strong fallen branches that you can wedge between other branches to make the platform. As you get more adventurous you can add sides and a top.

Tree houses are becoming a luxury commodity and you can see some amazing structures that have been built throughout the world. When we were at Wilderness Wood we found a book on luxury tree houses – real Nims Island fantasy living. We have a plan to make something like this one day. I have an idea we can build a series of platforms linked by rope swings and nets. Like Cosimo in Italo Calvino's *Baron in the Trees* you could actually lose yourself and stay up there for ever. Go up and never come down.

* Pine Marten
(Martes martes)

When we were staying in the far north-west of Scotland we were treated to the antics of the local Pine Martens that came to a bird food table outside the kitchen window. These beautiful, sleek animals with their bright yellowy-orange bibs were entrancing, jumping from rooftop to treetops and manoeuvring around the feeding table and tree. Every evening at teatime we would wait and watch these delightful creatures and their arboreal antics. A friend along the road said she leaves out peanut butter and jam for them. They can be quite destructive pests in these areas where they have lost their fear of humans.

Pine Martens are members of the mustelid family that includes Otters, Badgers and Weasels. They are largely confined to the coniferous forests of northern Scotland although there are isolated populations in the north of England. They are typically carnivorous taking small mammals, birds and insects but they will also eat berries, nuts and honey. They make their dens in hollow trees and holes in the ground and are predators of squirrels that they pursue acrobatically through the branches of the trees. Like the Otters, Pine Martens mark their territory with prominently placed scats. They usually mate in the summer but delayed implantation of the embryo means they do not give birth until early spring the following year. Usually between one and five young are born which are initially blind and bald. They are confined to the nest for three months and become independent at six months.

Balancing games – find your Zen

South Hams, Dartmoor

... Like Po, in Kung Fu Panda, I have achieved inner peace. I have become a master of Zen, for today, for the first time, I made it across the slack-rope. I took a deep breath right foot at hip height on the knot at the beginning of the line, I pushed up smoothly from the spongy leafy-litter keeping my body perfectly aligned and relaxed – in balance. After the push up I paused to gain my balance and move into the motion of the slack line. Before allowing myself to settle too much I transferred my weight forwards over the ball of my foot, arms floating out to the sides, legs flexed, my body responsive and ready to absorb the movement of the line. For a moment I felt completely poised and it flowed naturally, step followed step as my body relaxed and became as one with the line. I wasn't aware of any conscious thought, I was just moving in harmony, absorbing, bending and swaying with the movement of the slack line, focusing on a knot in the chestnut tree bark directly in front of me. My head felt clear and tranquil; the musty scent of the leaf litter and the song of the birds merged with the light breeze in the canopy resulting in a sense of weightlessness.

The sensation only lasted about twenty seconds and was gone as quickly as it arrived an intangible, irretrievable moment of flow. I had achieved inner peace. Then I was battling again, fighting to regain my balance and composure, clenching my core muscles desperately trying to recapture the relaxation and poise of moments before. Arms and spare leg flailing, the slack line swinging wildly from side to side as I am thrown off balance and over compensate in an effort to re-centre myself. Amazingly I hold on and gaining a semblance of balance make it to the other side – a moment of triumph. Now I have to have another go and see if I can do it again. It is so absorbing and addictive too ...

How to have fun with balance

Working on your balance is really good exercise. Although it is not aerobic – it won't provide much exercise for your heart and lungs – it is wonderful exercise for all your muscles and your mind.

The all important core muscles are worked hard as are your leg muscles. All the minor muscles in your feet and ankles that you were unaware of will be working overtime and the nerves linking the brain to your extremities are kept zinging with activity as messages are whizzed back and forth as they attempt to keep you balanced.

Working on your balance does wonders for your proprioception. Proprioception is the ability we have to sense movement in our own bodies. It tells us where each bit of our body is and how much muscle power is being used to keep it there and relies on the feedback system that our body uses to balance. If we step on uneven ground the receptors in our feet and ankles feed back to the brain so that the fine motor controls are readjusted and the muscles tighten appropriately to support our body at a different angle. Keeping these proprioceptors healthy is really important and will help protect you from trips and falls and twisted ankles.

When you twist your ankle you lose your proprioception as the nerves and muscles are damaged. Try to stand on a damaged ankle with your eyes closed and you may well just fall over. Try standing on a healthy ankle and you will feel all the minor adjustments that your ankle is making just to keep you upright. Apparently the reason adolescents going through growth spurts can be a bit clumsy and have more minor accidents than usual is due to a loss of proprioception as the body changes, this is quickly re-habituated if the person stays active.

You don't need to have a slack line to have fun with balance: all you need are some long thin poles. Consequently the woods are great for balancing games. Find a conveniently fallen tree, the longer and thinner the better. If it is wedged at about knee height that is fine but probably don't go too high if you want to try some of the harder challenges. As with all skills start simply and build up to become more challenging.

Start by standing on the trunk and walking along it. Once you have mastered a simple walk try some more challenges.

Here are a few to get you started:

● Bend down to touch the log
● Stand on one leg
● Do the yoga tree pose – stand on one leg, foot on knee and hands together above head
● Hop along the log
● Turn around and walk backwards
● Jump along the log
● Working with a partner walk towards each other join hands and try to swing past each other so that you can continue to walk along the log
● When you achieve your goal do a victory jump off the log – star jump or legs bent to the side – High School Musical style

••

If you fancy having a go at the slack rope yourself, a slack line is very easily set up with little equipment. A few metres of climbing tape and two climbing carabiners and you can set up anywhere you can find two strong trees a few metres apart. We now always take ours on holiday and it is absorbing entertainment for adults and children. If you want to know more there are some great YouTube clips and you can find all the equipment you need at any climbing shop. You can also buy dedicated slack lining kits, check out: needlesports.com, maverickslacklines. co.uk and gibbon-slacklines.com

North Downs Way, Surrey

... Today I've been introducing Team James Hill to a fiendish woodlands workout that I have devised along the North Downs Way.

Team James Hill was formed a few years ago when James Hill, a local Coldstream guard, was killed in Afghanistan. James' mum is a wonderful teacher at my children's infant school and in celebration of his life his colleagues, parents and fiancée organised an auction to raise money in his name. One of the prizes was a day out as a guardsman, which one of the mums bid for and won. Team James Hill, consisting of 11 mums plus James' parents and fiancée, were now committed to two months of intensive training. Starting from a mixed level of fitness we shuttle ran, skipped, press-upped, burpee-ed and dipped our way to fitness. The day as a guardsman was inspirational and emotional, we met James' battalion — guys who are on the front line for our country — took part in PT and weapons training, ate pack rations, did the team command challenges and then attacked the infamous Pirbright assault course while being bawled out by the PT instructor. By the end of the day we were exhausted and exhilarated but we all survived the experience with just a few colourful bruises and stiff muscles to live with.

These days the kids have moved on and are no longer at the school but Team James Hill keep in contact through less physically demanding nights out. But that had to change so I challenged them all to the woodland work out. It turned out to be the first recognisable day of spring after a disappointingly wet and cold start to the season. We started with a gentle jog and then moved on to some fiendishly tricky obstacles and challenges. In spite of lots of chatting it proved a good, full body work out. Some challenges were quite simple, some quite hard and some downright impossible. It was all fun and gave us food for thought for ongoing exercise entertainment ...

Some ideas for a woodland workout

There are many challenges you can set yourself on a woodland workout: use the trees and terrain as they present themselves. There will be sure to be some challenges to test your strength, flexibility, balance and footwork, for example:

If there are several of you many of these can be done as relays or performed as stop offs on a longer run or if you find several challenges in

USING FALLEN TREES

● Do shoulder presses and dead lifts by lifting the trunk
● Do log rolls rolling the trunk end over end
● Balance along them
● Do step ups

USING CLOSELY PLANTED TREES:

● Run a slalom through them
● Touch as many trees or a set number over a certain distance
● Climb, bridging between two trees

USING A SPRINGY BRANCH

● Depending on the height do shoulder presses, branch pull down, standing row or leg presses

ON A STATIC HORIZONTAL BRANCH

● Do chin ups
● Overhand crawl – monkey bars
● Hanging lift knees to elbows
● Up and over climb
● Limbo if it is quite low

BETWEEN TREE ROOTS

● Twinkle toes
● Bunny hops

ON A SLIM STANDING TREE

● Climb wrapping shins around the trunk
● Climb hands and feet on the trunk leaning back

one area so you can set up circuit training, moving between the stations for a minute (or appropriate set time) each.

Running in the woods is much more fun and better exercise than running on the roads with the challenges of uneven paths and the softer terrain, add in some ideas from the woodlands workout and you will give your whole body some exercise and have a bit of fun, even better, the dog can come too!

Stray off the path

Surrey Sculpture Park, Churt

... At the Sculpture Park today we found the most amazing installation:'The Black Box'. From the outside it just looked like a small shipping container. At the entrance was a sign warning you to enter quietly so as not to disturb the colony of endangered bats roosting inside and to keep to the left hand wall to avoid falling in holes. We entered in single file, with great trepidation, left hand on the wall, right hand extended back to the person behind. Moving forwards carefully we soon turned a corner and entered complete and utter blackness. You literally could not see the hand in front of your face – it was coal hole black. Stepping forwards into the unknown we expected the ground to fall away beneath our feet or bats to come screeching out at us at any moment. We followed the wall with our left hands going round corners, reaching dead ends and being lead out again, reaching the ends of walls and heading back down the other side. It seemed to go on forever until suddenly we turned a corner and saw light again and we were back at the opening. It was an illusion, a magic trick. Amazing. How could such a small container on the outside enclose such a large maze of terror and heightened awareness on the inside, with nothing but a few walls and complete darkness. We were transfixed and had to stay and try it out again and again to test our suspension of belief ...

Making the most of a small wood

Like 'The Black Box' small woodlands can give the same illusion of size and provide hours of fun in a relative small space. Particularly in summer when the curtains of greenery shield the sight lines and give views of only a few metres at a time it is a constant voyage of discovery with something new to see behind every tree. I went for a walk in a small wood near my sister's house. I walked around for about half an hour once popping out at a margin on a small lane that I didn't recognise at all. I returned into the wood for more wanderings and eventually found my way back to my starting point. When I looked on the map later the wood is no more than 400 sq m;

a bit of open land of that size would be passed over in a matter of minutes but a woodland creates an illusion and hides its contents away so you can search them out little by little.

Paths can lead you too quickly through the woodland, so stray off the path, follow your instinct and wander in small circles. Take a compass, set yourself a bearing and stick to it even through brambles and holly bushes, but follow a bearing rather than a path and see how much fun you can have in a small space. If it is small enough you don't need to worry about getting lost but if you are concerned, use your compass, your powers of observation or leave a trail like Hansel and Gretel.

Some
questions
answered

The deeper you look into the world of the woodland,
the more questions that will probably arise.
This section aims to shed light on a number of common
queries about trees and the woodland ecosystems.

How tall is that tree?

Trees are amazing organisms. They are by far the largest living things in the UK. They are heavier than any land animal and older than many ancient monuments. The statistics are staggering. A big oak or beech can weigh 30 tonnes, cover 2000 square yards and include 10 miles of twigs and branches. Each year the tree pumps several tonnes of water 100 feet into the air, produces a new crop of 100,000 leaves and covers half an acre of trunk and branches with a new layer of bark (Pakenham 2003). Standing back and surveying the majesty of a fully-grown tree it is very hard to get an idea of how tall they are.

The most accurate measure used by tree specialists is to climb right to the top of the tree and drop a rope down until it reaches the ground. You then measure the length of the rope and hence the height of the tree. The trouble with this method is that trees are very high and it is very hard to climb right to the top of a tree. Assuming that you do not possess the equipment to safely climb a tree to make a direct height measurement

then how else will you be able measure, or estimate its height?

There are several indirect techniques that can be used to measure or estimate the height of a tree. All of the techniques have some basis in maths, relying rely on our understanding of proportion, ratios or trigonometry, but don't worry they are very simple.

Proportion measurements

THUMBS UP MEASURE

I found this technique on YouTube. It is both simple and works really well. Walk away from a tree with your arm outstretched and thumbs up. When your thumb reaches the top of the tree and the base of your hand the base of the tree stop. Rotate your hand to horizontal with the base of your hand still on the base of the tree. Get a friend to stand at the point where your thumb tip is and then measure the distance from your friend to the base of the tree. This will give you the height of your tree.

The only problem with this technique can sometimes be your ability to get far enough away from the tree for the tree to fit your thumb. To solve this problem just take a stick, hold at arms length and mark off or break at the tree height. Then turn the stick horizontally with the mark at the base of the tree, get a friend to stand at the tip of the stick and measure as before.

SHADOW MEASUREMENTS

For this technique you will need a solid object whose length you know accurately – ideally a metre rule; a piece of string; and probably the most limiting factor, a sunny day. Place the metre rule, or yourself on the ground and measure its shadow – you can do this with a length of string – this is a shadow metre. At the same time or as soon afterwards as possible, mark where the tree's shadow is on the ground. Then using your string shadow metre measure the length of the tree shadow and you will get the tree height. If you don't have a metre ruler but you know your own height you can use your own shadow and calculate the tree height from that.

Make a simple clinometer

Cut a paper plate in half and half way along
it hang a piece of string weighted with a
stone or other small heavy object. Mark on
the plate a 45° angle. You can do this with a
protractor or by folding the plate to find
the half and then quarter fold (if half a
circle is a 90° angle then a quarter of a
circle is 45°). Looking along the edge of the
plate, line it up with the top of the tree.
Walk away from the tree until the edge of
the plate is lined up with the tree and the
string is hanging directly down the 45°
angle line. The height of the tree is the
distance away from the tree that you are
plus your height. So if you are 1.5m tall and
you find yourself 10m away from the tree,
it is 11.5m tall.

RATIO MEASUREMENT

I have found this technique less accurate than
the ones above simply because there are too
many measurements where errors can creep in.
However, it is worth a try.

    Take a 30cm ruler or measure a 30cm piece of
card and mark 3cm from the bottom. Walk away
from the tree with the card at arms length until
the top of the tree is in line with the top of the
card and the bottom at the base of the tree. Next
get a helper to move their hand up the trunk of
the tree until it is directly in line with the 3cm
mark on the ruler or the 3cm mark on the card.
Then measure the height of their hand from the
ground. Since 3cm is 1/10 of the length of piece of
paper multiply the distance from ground to hand
by 10 and you have the height of the tree.

TRIGONOMETRY CALCULATIONS

After a direct measurement tree specialists will
often employ a gauge called a clinometer to
measure tree height. The clinometer uses the
knowledge that the angles in a triangle always
add up to 180°. So a triangle with a right angle –
90° – at its top and one other angle at 45° must
have a third angle of 45°. So, if we look at the top
of the tree from a 45° angle our distance from the
tree will be the height of the tree plus the height
from the ground that we are observing from.

    You can buy clinometers and may well have
used one at school. There are even clinometer
apps you can get for smartphones. The most
important feature of the clinometer is to ensure
that you are looking at the top of your tree at an
angle of 45°.

You will often hear people talking about a tree species as being native or non-native but what does that actually mean?

The first trees found on earth were the ancestors of the conifers that developed from vascular plants around 340 million years ago in the late carboniferous period. Prior to this, giant tree ferns and horsetails dominated the upper storey of forests. In the Jurassic period around 140 million years ago the broadleaved trees evolved from the fern trees while the currently recognised genera of trees finally evolved in the Palaeocene around 70 million years ago. That is still some 67.5 million years before the hominids that arrived 2.5 million years ago. The present human species – *Homo sapiens* – has been around just 200,000 years and the last great Ice Age ended around 10,000 years ago and it was as the ice retreated and our present day trees colonised the land that we consider modern woodland history in Britain begins.

Botanists define 'native trees' as those trees that colonised Britain after the last Ice Age without human assistance and before we were cut off from continental Europe.

As the ice retreated northwards the heavily compressed northern lands bounced up from the release of the weight and in counterbalance the southern lands tipped down. The glaciers retreated at a rate of roughly half a mile a year or

50 miles a century (Macfarlane, 2007) and as the ice retreated sea levels rose. The water released from the glaciers created great rivers that eventually inundated the land bridge of chalk that had joined Britain to Europe. By a point around 10,000 years ago the ice had retreated to near enough its current position and Britain was cut off from the rest of Europe. Our land became covered by new woodland – willow, birch and pine leading on to oak, lime, Ash, Hazel, Hornbeam and scrub.

There are around 33 species of tree that are normally considered to be natives. All other trees are foreigners!

Those that grow biggest and live longest are generally our most cherished trees and these include the Common and Sessile Oak, Ash, beech, Silver and Downy birch, Yew and Scots Pine. The other 25 are:

Alder

Box

Aspen

Juniper

Small-leaved Lime

Bird Cherry

Large-leaved Lime

Blackthorne

Field Maple

Crab Apple

Black Poplar

Wild or Gean Cherry

Crack Willow

Starwberry Tree (Ireland only)

Bay Willow

Wych Elm

Goat Willow

Common Hawthorne

White Willow

Midland Hawthorne

Hazel

Hornbeam

Rowan or Mountain Ash

Holly

Wild Service

There is much dispute over which species are native and non-native. The English and Field Elms are often included in lists of native species, however, they are under dispute as they may have been introduced by Bronze Age farmers. There is further debate over which are naturalised historic species (i.e. introduced some time ago – conventionally pre-1500 AD) like the Sweet Chestnut or a modern introduction like the Sycamore. The Sweet Chestnut is thought to have been introduced by the Romans so qualifies as a naturalised historic species and has been taken into our affections as a surrogate native. The much-maligned Sycamore, by contrast, is almost treated as a weed, it is currently quite frowned on by conservationists as being ecologically inferior and this affects its acceptability and image as a naturalised species. However, if earlier records of sycamore can be found it may be 'promoted' to a historic rather than modern introduced species.

List compiled from various sources – Woodland Trust, Julian Hight, Royal Forestry Society

What is 'ancient woodland'?

Ancient woodland is woodland that is known to have existed pre 1600 – around the era of Elizabeth I. This date has been chosen because it was during this time that reliable and widespread estate records started to be kept. It is also believed that our history of plantations began at around this time. This means that woods identified in estate records from this period are considered to be naturally sown woodlands even if they were extensively managed.

Ancient woodlands are special because they have stood on the same soil for at least 500 years. This creates a very stable environment and the very particular plant associations they contain and consequently the wildlife they attract.

To check out if a wood is ancient or not you can either search back through estate records from the 1600 or look in the Ancient Woodland Inventory held by Natural England (England's statutory conservation agency) and produced by the Nature Conservancy in the 1980s and 1990s. However, if you find yourselves in a wood without access to the Ancient Woodland Inventory could you tell if you are in ancient woodland or not by looking around you?

The most well documented method of identifying ancient woodland is to look at the plant associations. Certain plants act as indictors of ancient woodland. The more of these that are

Foxglove

Foxglove

Wood anemone

Bluebell

Ramsons (wild garlic)

present the greater confidence you can have that you are actually in ancient woodland. You must be aware that the list of indicators varies from region to region. For example: bluebells in southern England are indicators of ancient woodland but in Cornwall they often grow in hedgerows unrelated to ancient woodland sites. It is necessary to look at the lists of indicators for your region and assess your woodland accordingly.

Full lists of indicator species for each region can be found at the Natural History Museum website www.nhm.ac.uk

Common ancient woodland indicators to look out for include:

Woodruff

Wood anemone

Bluebell   Yellow archangel

Wild strawberry   Oxlip

Primrose   Herb paris

Lily of the Valley

Wood spurge

Wood forget me not   Ransoms

Greater stitchwort

Wood sorrel

Yellow pimpernel

It is almost impossible to create ancient woodland. The native tree woodland we planted on my grandparent's land is now around 35 years old. It is growing well and is attracting its own wildlife, however, it is still a long way from supporting the rich diversity of an ancient woodland site. The Woodland Trust identifies 150,000ha of ancient woodland in the UK, mostly in lowland England but there used to be much more. Around 350,000ha were destroyed around the time of the First and Second World Wars between 1910 and 1950. At this point they were replanted with conifer plantations as a commercial crop, this policy is now seen as a mistake and that trend is now being reversed in favour of native mixed woodland.

Planting trees on old agricultural land will take a long time to approximate ancient woodland. So while planting trees is a great thing to do there is really no substitute for ancient woodland, we must remember that when we see them under threat from development. Once gone ancient woodlands are gone.

What kills trees?

No tree is immortal. At some point all trees will die, even if few actually survive to reach old age and just crumble away. The slower growing trees tend to live to greater ages and all have different typical lifespans.

The oak is said to grow for 300 years, be in its prime for 300 years and die off for 300 years – some ancient specimens are believed to be 1000years old. In contrast an 80-year-old birch has reached a good age. The Yew is the real grandfather of our native trees with some ancient individuals believed to date back 4000 years.

It is actually very hard to kill a tree. Even the most dead looking stump will suddenly produce shoots from its base and like a phoenix rising from the ashes develop into a new tree. However, there are a number of factors that will produce stress in a tree that can eventually combine to kill it off.

Cutting down trees

People often believe that when you cut a tree down it dies. This is true of conifer trees, however, the majority of deciduous trees will shoot again from a cut stump or from the roots underground. A tree can be cut back quite aggressively every few years and will continue to send up new shoots for many centuries. This ability to re-shoot has been exploited in woodland management for centuries through the process of coppicing. This technique can increase the longevity of a tree by many years if not centuries. A coppiced Ash for example, can live for 800 years but would usually fall to pieces at around 200 years if left to its own devices (Rackham 2006).

Burning trees

In hot climates woodlands have evolved alongside fire; the trees are adapted to withstand fire and the fire clears the undergrowth and stimulates the trees germination. Fire can stimulate the growth of smaller plants in a similar manner to coppicing. In general fire will not kill trees and clear woodland but will open up the ground a bit to provide better grazing land between the trees.

Our native woodlands don't burn well; their damp, mulchy leaf litter resists the heat so the fire is unable to take hold on the large trunks that will not burn on their own. Planted conifer woodlands are a risk packed as they are with bracken and dry grass. Similarly, individual native trees surrounded by bracken or heather are also at greater risk, and there are many incidences where vandalism has killed ancient trees when people have set fires in the base of their hollows.

Die back and dead branches

All old trees will show some die back. This is a technique that trees employ to enable them to live longer. Branches formed when the tree was young and are now no longer needed, will die off and may be dropped. In oaks, unnecessary branches and diseased or damaged wood is sectioned off by altering a layer of wood that becomes impregnated with tannins. The branches are effectively bypassed when the tree is under stress from drought or predation by insects or fungi; the tree protects itself by killing off a few superfluous branches in its crown allowing the rest of the tree to continue to grow. Dead boughs remain to giving the characteristic 'stag headed' oaks which become features in the landscape. The oak can therefore remain otherwise healthy and unchanged for a century or more in this state.

A big tree often goes hollow in old age; this is again a survival mechanism, a cylinder being a very strong structure and the central wood no longer being needed for growth. The strength of these hollow trees was evident in the high winds of the Great Storm of 1987. The most damaged trees were the younger trees that had reached full height but not full girth. Relatively few of the really old hollow trees fell.

Grazing

The increase in deer numbers is putting trees under a greater strain than in the past. Grazing animals (deer, sheep, cows but also rabbits and squirrels) can be devastating to young tree growth. In managed woodlands grazing animals are usually kept out in the first years after coppicing to allow regrowth. Grazers have much less of an impact on established trees. Even on young trees they will often not kill off the plant. They may stunt its growth resulting in stumps that will wait until the grazers have gone and then take their chance to sprout later. The greater damage is caused to the understory plants that will be grazed out leaving trees and grassland rather than a well-developed woodland ecology.

Trees can suffer periodically from infestations of caterpillars that can defoliate a tree and limit growth for that year. Usually an abundance one year will be tempered with a couple of years of low numbers allowing the tree to grow well in those years, so the long term effects are usually sustainable.

Diseases

The vast majority of tree diseases are insignificant. Trees can survive for years and probably are afflicted by a number of minor diseases and parasites. The effect may be just enough to slow down their growth but nothing more serious.

A burden of disease in trees is quite normal but how much is sustainable for the tree and how much is 'normal' is a difficult question. Certain diseases have caused devastating epidemics that have decimated individual tree species. Probably the most notorious is the Dutch Elm Disease (DED). This disease flared up in the 1960s and within 20 years had killed 90 per cent of elms in England (Rackham 2006). Recent concerns over Ash die back are anticipating similar devastating impacts on Ash trees.

In fact few of the elms were killed completely by DED and have sent out shoots from the roots and stumps and regrown, often to be re-infected when they reach maturity.

Combined factors

It is often a combination of factors that will finally kill off a tree. Several winters of frost, combined with heavy grazing by animals that can reach high into the tree, as well as a honey fungus in the roots of a tree, may be enough to kill a tree off where the effect of each might have been quite insignificant.

The weakening effect of a parasitic fungus may be the final twig to break the oaks back. Trees are incredibly hard to kill. You have to be quite persistent to actually get rid of a woodland. The only way to do it effectively is to keep at it year after year. Digging out the stumps and cultivating the soil is the only sure way to clear woodland. Any land left untended for a length of time will find itself colonised by trees.

What is tree time?

Like geological time where the cycling of rocks depositing and weathering carries on over long timescales, trees have a much longer, slower life cycle than ours and operate under 'tree time'. 'If an oak takes 50 years to produce its first acorns, evolution acts 200-fold more slowly than on mice', the implications of this in our rapidly changing world are a bit of a worry. Humans have speeded up environmental change like a flickering old black and white movie. Whether the slow moving timescales of the old oak and even older yew – adapted to environmental conditions in prehistory – can keep up with these superimposed changes is a whole new challenge for evolution and natural selection.

We often cause a problem for trees because they are introduced to changes at human speed – a much faster rate than nature would operate in tree time. A disease that enters a woodland naturally through wind and animal vectors would typically arrive and spread quite slowly. Trees, plants and animals would have a chance to adapt and develop their own defence mechanisms. Confronted with the assault of disease imported in large numbers by humans, the native stocks have little time to develop immunity and the danger of whole species being wiped out is much more real.

In the same way that different species of mammals have very different lifespans; the largest land mammals, the elephant, can live for 70 years while voles only live for one to two years; different species of tree will also have different lifespans.

The size of the species and the speed at which it grows both influence the longevity of a tree species. Within species the growing conditions to

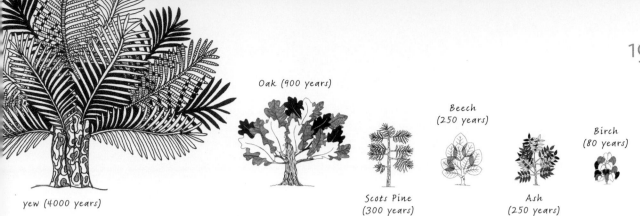

Oak (900 years)

Beech
(250 years)

Birch
(80 years)

yew (4000 years)

Scots Pine
(300 years)

Ash
(250 years)

which it is exposed will also have an influence, so a fast growing tree will reach the end of its life much more quickly than its slow growing relative. A big broad oak lives longer than a slim birch and a stunted hawthorn growing sideways on a mountain is often much older than its faster growing southern hedge relative. The bristle cone pines growing in the deserts of California grow extremely slowly; the oldest living specimens are over 5000 years old with a trunk often of no more than 3m in diameter – an oak of similar diameter would be just 150 years old – a mere infant.

Each species of tree will have a typical lifespan. The ages above are based on typical un-pollarded or coppiced ages – there may be some ancient specimens that exceed the typical ages substantially.

A pollarded or coppiced tree can live for much longer than an uncut tree as the process of coppicing keeps the tree in its juvenile state so that it never reaches maturity and therefore never dies. The coppiced stool may be very old but the individual stems are never older than the length of the last cutting cycle.

Deciduous woodlands have much greater biodiversity value in this country than the monoculture pinewoods that are often planted for forestry purposes. However, the natural coniferous woodlands of Scotland, remnants of the great Caledonian Forest, are extremely diverse habitats that support a whole range of plants and animals in their communities.

The nature of a woodland is dictated, in part, by the dominant tree species growing in it. Just consider one factor, the amount of light that is captured by the different tree species and hence the amount of light that reaches the woodland floor. A birch wood may allow as much as 50 per cent of the incident light through its canopy while oak woodland allows 20 per cent of light through and beech only allows 5 per cent. These differences account for the plant assemblages seen in the shrub, field and ground layers of birch, oak and beech dominated woodland. The understory in beech woodlands is much clearer than that in a birch or oak woodland. Pine plantations are even further down this scale. The canopy is closed and dense and very little light

reaches the forest floor so there is almost no understory.

Our eyes adapt very well to changing light conditions and it can be hard to appreciate how low the light levels are in beech woodlands in summer. To fully appreciate how much light is coming through the leaves try taking activity photos – even in a birch woodland in mid-summer it can be hard to get enough light. Trick your eyes by running into woodland; before your eyes have time to adjust to the low light levels you can actually appreciate the lack of light.

Aside from the dominant tree species and the effect they have on light levels another extremely important factor affecting diversity in woodlands is the nature of the soils. Ancient woodlands show such high levels of diversity because their soils have been undisturbed for over 500 years. Modern woodmen go to extreme lengths to avoid disturbing soils any more than is necessary when they are coppicing because they know that one of the most damaging factors of forestry is the disturbance of the soils caused by periodic felling and removal of the wood. All

woodland soils are acidic due to leaf decay but the persistence of the needles in conifer woodlands means they are particularly so. Deciduous woodlands tend to be acidic at the surface due to the leaf litter; however, the action of earthworms can counteract this. Earthworms can only operate in soils with a of more than 4 that are known as mull soils. Earthworms cannot tolerate lower pHs than this and so the soils become leaf-mulch dominated and progressively more acidic.

Diversity in conifer woodlands

Pine plantations are monocultures that are grown purely for the harvest of wood. They are comparable to arable fields in their diversity and value as conservation areas and should be considered accordingly. The main problems are that the trees are planted very densely so prevent light reaching the forest floor, all the trees are of the same age and height and are regularly felled causing a disturbance to the forest floor. Tree thinning takes place but no logs are left to rot so there are no decomposers and no base to the food chain. The only inputs to the soils are the persistent needles that decay very slowly producing acidic soils that are not favourable to other flora and fauna. Like field margins and hedgerows on agricultural land, the most important areas of a plantation forest for wildlife are the firebreaks. These open corridors allow in light, they are well protected from high winds and have stable temperatures, and typically support a good diversity of acidic grassland or heathland species.

The Caledonian Forest is made up of conifer woodlands dominated by the Scots Pine,

however, it is not a monoculture in the way that plantations are, so other tree species such as birch and aspen are mixed in and break up the canopy. The Scots Pine forests are the only true habitat of the Pine Marten and the Crossbill that feeds extensively on the pinecones; Scottish Wildcats and Red Squirrels also live there. Unlike the conifer plantations the trees grow to maturity and have a wide range of associated species, including epiphytic lichen and mosses much like the broad leafed woodlands. While the usual processes of limb drop and decay occur, the dominance of needles in the leaf litter and year round leaf cover still results in an acidic soil and an impoverished understory when compared to deciduous woodland.

Diversity in broadleaf woodlands

In deciduous woodlands, even beech woodland, the tree canopy is only truly closed from the end of May through the summer months. The understory gets its moment in the light in spring and this is the most prolific time for flowering species and their associated fauna. The summer months are dominated by activity in the canopy both for plants and animals, while the autumn sees activity both in the canopy as the trees seed and nut harvest takes off, as well as in the ground layer as the leaves fall and the fungi proliferate.

Cycling through the seasons in broadleaf woodland, flora and fauna flourish in all levels throughout the wood from the soils through the ground layer, the field and shrub layers and into the canopy. This stratification and layering of communities in woodlands allows for a high-rise effect of diversity. Where open grassland is limited to two layers of communities the woodland supports four or five layers leading to a much greater density of flora and fauna for the same footprint. The extremely high levels of diversity on oak trees are accounted for by the fact that even the bark supports communities of plants and animals feeding on the epiphytic mosses and lichens. No niche is left unexploited by the tree.

Kett's Oak, Wymondham, Norfolk

... Trees can live a long time. It is hardly conceivable that some Yew trees have been living in one spot for up to 4000 years. Even an old oak of up to 1000 years has seen some immense changes throughout its life. At school in Norfolk we were always taught about Kett's Rebellion. Kett was a tanner and landowner who led a rebellion against the crown, of some 20,000 rebels enraged by the enclosure of common land. This was an important point in Norfolk history and Norwich Castle, which the rebels initially captured, has a plaque honouring Kett that tells you about the rebellion and his ultimate hanging. The fact that Kett rallied his men beside an oak tree that still stands just outside Wymondham really brings home the history that these great trees have lived through.

The tree below is modelled on Kett's Oak and illustrates the changes that a tree of such longevity will have lived through ...

- 1066 Battle of Hastings
- 1086 Domesday Book produced
- 1145 Norwich Cathedral completed
- 1215 Signing of the Magna Carta
- 1381 The Peasants' Revolt led to the abolition of serfdom
- 1485 The Battle of Bosworth ended the
Wars of the Roses and heralded the reign of the Tudors
- 1509 Henry VIII comes to the throne
- 1549 Kett's Rebellion
- 1588 The Spanish Armada
- 1665 The Great Plague
- 1666 The Fire of London
- 1651 English Civil War – King Charles II hides
in an oak tree to escape Puritan forces
- 1760+ Start of the Industrial Revolution
- 1739 The Wesley Brothers preach to ordinary
people from under trees
- 1885 The internal combustion engine changes
the face of Britain
- 1903 The Wright Brothers make their first flight over Britain
- 1914-45 The First and Second World Wars
- 1969 The first man walks on the moon
- 1987 The Great Storm: an estimated 15 million trees fall in one night
- 2012 The Queen's Golden Jubilee: six million trees
planted across the UK

Resources

Finding woodland to visit

The Woodland Trust
www.woodlandtrust.org.uk and
www.visitwoods.org.uk

The Forestry Commission
www.forestry.gov.uk

The Wildlife Trusts
www.wildlifetrusts.org

Local Wildlife Trusts
Local wildlife trusts are usually in the
format of *www.surreywildlifetrust.org*

National Trust
www.nationaltrust.org.uk

Arboreta and botanical gardens to visit

Wikipedia has a link page to any
botanical garden, arboretum and
pinetum in the UK
*http://en.wikipedia.org/wiki/List_of_
botanical_gardens_in_the_United_
Kingdom*

Ancient woodland

LISTS OF INDICATOR SPECIES
Natural History Museum
www.nhm.ac.uk

ANCIENT WOODLAND INVENTORIES
Natural England
www.naturalengland.org.uk

Scottish Natural Heritage
www.snh.gov.uk

Countryside Council for Wales
www.ccw.gov.uk

Identification guides

TREES
The Woodland Trust and
www.british-trees.com

Field Studies Council fold out guide The
Tree Name Trail: A key to common trees

Collins: Complete Guide to British Trees

FUNGI
Collins: Fungi Guide

Field Studies Council fold out guide: The
Fungi Name Trail – A key to commoner
fungi

LICHENS
British Lichens, incorporating a species
guide:
www.britishlichens.co.uk

MAMMALS
Field Studies Council fold out guide:
A Guide to British Mammals Tracks and
Signs

BIRDSONG
Collins: Bird Songs and Calls CD

British Library: Beautiful Bird Songs of
Britain CD

BBC: A Guide to British Woodland Birds
CD

Royal Society for the Protection of Birds:
www.RSPB.org.uk

The web magazine for birdwatchers:
www.birdsofbritain.co.uk

Sculpture parks

Birkbeck University of London has an
International Directory of sculpture
parks and gardens
http://www.bbk.ac.uk/sculptureparks/

Green Man

**Countryfile Magazine's map of Green
Man Locations UK**
*www.countryfile.com/countryside/
green-man-map*

Slacklines

www.needlesports.com
www.gibbon-slacklines.com
www.maverickslacklines.co.uk

Tree canopy access

**RECREATIONAL TREE CLIMBING
TRAINING**
Treefrog Climbing Adventures
www.treefrogclimbing.co.uk

TREE CLIMBING EQUIPMENT
www.honeybros.co.uk

New Tribe Tree Hammocks
www.newtribe.com

TREE TOP ADVENTURE COURSES
Go Ape *www.goape.co.uk*

www.ttadventure.co.uk and many other
high ropes adventure courses.

CANOPY WALKS
Royal Botanical Gardens, Kew
www.kew.org

Salcey Forest Centre
www.forestry.gov.uk/salceyforest

LIVING TREE DESIGNS
Richard Reames
www.arborsmith.com

Peter Cook
www.pooktre.com

TREE FESTIVALS AND FAIRS

The Festival of the Tree at Westonbirt
www.forestry.gov.uk/westonbirt-treefest

Woodfest Wales
www.woodfestwales.co.uk

The Yorkshire Arboretum
www.wildaboutwood.org

Weald Woodfair
www.bentley.org.uk/#/events-september/4533778606

The Woodland Trust advertises fairs and festivals at its sites
www.woodlandtrust.org

Listings of wood fairs throughout the UK can be found at
www.woodfairs.co.uk

World Conker Championships
www.worldconkerchampionships.com

General interest

Wild About Britain
www.wildaboutbritain.co.uk

Forest Schools
www.forestschools.com

Beautiful pictures of trees, forests and woods
www.treeporn.net

A record of life on earth
www.arkive.org

Other

The Tree Council
www.treecouncil.org.uk

The Royal Forestry Society
www.rfs.org.uk

I have had a great time researching and writing this book and my sincerest thanks must go to a whole host of people who have helped make the process so much fun. Firstly I must thank all my family. From my long suffering husband Duncan who, I think, has enjoyed the tree climbing and mega-swing activities as much as the kids and has entered into the whole woodland experience with great enthusiasm. My girls, Anousha, Thea, Poppy and Lottie, who provide never ending fun and inspiration in their enjoyment of the woods and of course Alfie who has accompanied me on many long days running and walking, climbing and photographing, generally behaving impeccably and waiting patiently.

All the rest of my family have been a great source of information and anecdote as well as being part of so many woodland days. Thank you to the Turner clan; Mum, Ruth, Chris and Ian, Mark, Katie, Al, Hannah, Rachael, Jacob, Mollie, Lizzie, Diggory, Sam, Tim and Abes (not forgetting Alfie's friends Nutmeg, Sona and Oscar); and the Wardley clan Bryan and Cynthia, Gavin, Genna, Aaron and Samara.

Friends have played a big part in the writing of this book in their general support as well as being guinea pigs, providing photos, experiences, inspiration and company. Particular thanks go to: Morwenna, who cast an eye over an early draft, the Hudsons, Almonds, Merrys, Hassans, Perfitts, McDowalls, Eastlakes, Van Duijns, Rigneys, Seerajs and Team James Hill.

Special thanks go to Roland from Treefrog who taught Dunc and I how to climb trees and opened up a whole new world for us.

Holmesdale School Eco Club provided a rich source of entertainment, so thanks to Sara Richards, fellow leader and Sarah Beasley, head teacher who embraced or at least tolerated my ideas and allowed me to try them out on the enthusiastic guinea pigs, sorry, kids who came along with no idea of what they were about to do. Thanks also to Mr Moses at Reigate Priory School who allowed Poppy to write about his game of thicket and for all the great days my kids have had at the school in their outdoor education.

It also goes without saying that this book would not have happened without the input of Bloomsbury Publishing in particular my editor Lisa Thomas and designer Nicola Liddiard.

Bibliography

Adams, D. 1979. *The Hitchhiker's Guide to the Galaxy.* Pan

Almond, D. 1998. *Skellig.* Hodder

Almond, D. 2012. *My Name is Mina.* Yearling Books.

Blyton, E. 2008. *The Magic Faraway Tree Collection.* Egmont

Calvino, I. 1977. *The Baron in the Trees.* Thompson Learning.

Colling, W. 2005. *D is for Dahl.* Puffin Books.

Deakin, R. 2008. *Notes from Walnut Tree Farm.* Penguin Books.

Deakin, R. 2008. *Wildwood, A Journey Through Trees.* Penguin Books.

Dennis, F. 2010. *Tales from the Woods.* Ebury Press.

Doell, F and G. 2001. *The Green Man in Britain.* The History Press Ltd.

Gooley, T. 2010. *The Natural Navigator.* Virgin Books.

Goscinny, R. and Uderzo, A. 2005. *Asterix the Gaul.* Hachette Livre.

Hight, J. 2011. *Britain's Tree Story: the history and legends of Britain's ancient trees.* National Trust Books.

Holland, C. 2012. *I Love My World.* Wholeland Press.

Johnson, H. 2010. *Trees: a lifetime's journey through forests, woods, and gardens.* Mitchell Beazley.

Kieran, D. and Hodgkinson, T. 2008. *The Book of Idle Pleasures.* Ebury Press.

Kromer, B. 2009. 'Radiocarbon and Dendrochronology'. *Dendrochronologia* 27, 15–19.

Law, B. 2008. *The Woodland Year.* Permanent Publications.

Lear, E. 2012. *The Owl and the Pussycat.* Templar Books.

Mabey, R. 2010. *A Brush With Nature.* BBC Books.

Mabey, R. 2011. *The Perfumier and The Stinkhorn.* Profile Books.

MacFarlane, R. 2012. *The Old Ways.* Hamish Hamilton.

MacFarlane, R. 2007. *The Wild Places.* Granta Publications.

Martel Y. 2002. *Life of Pi.* Canongate Books

Milne A.A. 1973. *The World of Pooh.* Methuen Children's Books

Molteno, S., Morris, J. and O'Brien, L. 2012. 'Public access to woodlands and forests: a rapid evidence review'. *Forest Research.* Forestry Commission

Pakenham, T. 2003. *Meetings with Remarkable Trees.* Weidenfeld & Nicholson.

Peterken, G. F. 1996. *Natural Woodland: ecology and conservation in northern temperate regions.* Cambridge University Press.

Pouyet, M. 2006. *Natural, Simple Land Art Through the Seasons.* Frances Lincoln.

Price, D. 2000. The Moonlight Chronicles: a wandering artist's journal. Ten Speed Press.

Rackham, O. 2006. *Woodlands.* Collins.

Rowling, J K. 1997. *Harry Potter and the Philosopher's Stone.* Bloomsbury.

Scottish Land Reform Act 2003

Shepherd, N. 2011. *The Living Mountain.* Canongate.

The Countryside Rights of Way Act 2000

Thomas, P.A. and Packham, J.R. 2007. *Ecology of Woodlands and Forests.* Cambridge University Press.

Tolkien, J.R.R. 2009. *The Hobbit.* Harper Collins

Tolkien, J.R.R. 1999. *The Lord of the Rings.* Harper Collins

Tudge, A. 2005. *The Secret Life of Trees.* Allen and Lane.

White, T.H. 1958. *The Once and Future King.* Collins

Woodland Trust 2010. 'Space for People: targeting action for woodland access'. Woodland Trust: Grantham